The Masonic Book Club

—————— Vol. 1 ——————

The Regius Poem

Westphalia Press
An Imprint of the Policy Studies Organization
Washington, DC

The Regius Poem

All Rights Reserved © 2025 by Policy Studies Organization

Westphalia Press
An imprint of Policy Studies Organization
1367 Connecticut Avenue NW
Washington, D.C. 20036
info@ipsonet.org

ISBN: 978-1-63723-546-1

Daniel Gutierrez-Sandoval, Executive Director
PSO and Westphalia Press

Updated material and comments on this edition
can be found at the Westphalia Press website:
www.westphaliapress.org

The Masonic Book Club

The *Masonic Book Club* (MBC) was formed in 1970 by two Illinois Masons, Alphonse Cerza, 33°, and Louis L. Williams, 33°. The MBC primarily reprinted out-of-print Masonic books with scholarly introductions; occasionally they would print additional texts as "bonuses" (though none were marked specifically as such on the title pages); sometimes a reprint would be marked "Masonic Book Club Edition"; often an unnumbered bonus was published jointly with the Illinois Lodge of Research or the Supreme Council, 33°, NMJ, USA.

Most of the MBC volumes indicated on the title page, "Volume [*Number*] of the Publications of the Masonic Book Club," some were misnumbered, and some were unnumbered. Indeed, the numbering of the early volumes was inconsistent. For example, *A Serious and Impartial Enquiry* is "Volume Five" (1974) but *Masonic Membership of the Founding Fathers* is "The Masonic Book Club Edition" (1974). Then, *Masonry Dissected* is "Volume Eight" (1977), *The Trestleboard* is "Volume 8A" (1978), and *Anderson's Constitutions of 1738* is "Volume Nine" (1978). If nothing else, MBC books keep bibliophiles on their toes.

The first volumes had deckle-edged paper and pages of slightly different sizes, though eventually the MBC settled into a 6″×9″ trimmed-page format for their books. The books were bound in a dark blue fabric with gold lettering. Listed below are the fifty-nine MBC volumes published 1970–2010 with bonuses. N.B.: A number and letter, e.g. "Volume 8A," is a numbering for this reprint series.

The club originally was limited to 333 members, but the number grew to nearly 2,000, with 1,083 members when it dissolved in 2010. In 2017 MW Barry Weer, 33°, the last president of the MBC, transferred the MBC name and assets to the Supreme Council, 33°, SJ, USA. Under the editorship of Arturo de Hoyos, 33°, G∴C∴, and S. Brent Morris, 33°, G∴C∴, the revived Masonic Book Club has the goal of publishing classic Masonic books while supporting Scottish Rite, SJ, USA philanthropies.

Publications of the Masonic Book Club, 1970–2010

1	1970	*The Regius Poem*	Masonic Book Club
2	1971	*The Constitutions of the Free-Masons*	Benjamin Franklin
3	1972	*Ahiman Rezon*	Laurence Dermott
4	1973	*Illustrations of Masonry*	William Preston
5	1974	*A Serious and Impartial Enquiry into the Cause of the Present Decay of Free-Masonry in the Kingdom of Ireland*	Fifield D'Assigny
5A	1974*	*Masonic Membership of the Founding Fathers*	Ronald E. Heaton

6	1975	*The Signers of the Declaration of Independence*	David C. Whitney
7	1976	*The Signers of the Constitution of the United States*	David C. Whitney
7A	1976*	*Masonic Symbols in American Decorative Art*	Louis L. Williams & Alphonse Cerza
8	1977	*Samuel Prichard's Masonry Dissected, 1730*	Harry Carr
8A	1978*	*Trestle-Board (A facsimile of the original Trestle Board by the Baltimore Masonic Convention of 1843)*	Dwight L. Smith
9	1978	*Anderson's Constitutions of 1738*	Lewis Edward & W. J. Hughan
10	1979	*Sufferings of John Coustos*	Wallace McLeod
11	1980	*The Revelations of a Square*	George Oliver
11A	1980	*Biblical Characters in Freemasonry*	John H. Van Gorden
11B	1980*	*A Masonic Reader's Guide*	*Guide* Alphonse Cerza & Thomas Warden
12	1981	*Three Distinct Knocks and Jachin and Boaz*	Harry Carr
13	1982	*Masonic Almanacs and Anti-Masonic Almanacs*	Plez A. Transou
13A	1982*	*Stephen A. Douglas: Freemason*	Wayne C. Temple
14	1983	*The Beginnings of Freemasonry in America*	Melvin M. Johnson
14A	1983*	*Bespangled, Painted & Embroidered: Decorated Masonic Aprons in America, 1790–1850*	Scottish Rite Masonic Museum & Library
14B	1983*	*Making a Mason at Sight*	Louis L. Williams
15	1984	*Masonic Concordance of the Holy Bible*	Charles Clyde Hunt
15A	1984*	*By Square and Compasses: The Building of Lincoln's Home and Its Saga*	Wayne C. Temple

16	1985	*The Old Gothic Constitutions*	Wallace McLeod
16A	1985*	*Modern Historical Characters in Freemasonry*	John H. Van Gorden
17	1986	*The Rise and Development of Organised Freemasonry*	Roy A. Wells
17A	1986*	*Ancient and Early Medieval Historical Characters in Freemasonry*	John H. Van Gorden
18	1987	*The Lodge in Friendship Village and Other Stories*	P. W. George
18A	1987*	*Masonic Charities*	John H. Van Gorden & Stewart M. L. Pollard
18B	1987*	*Medieval Historical Characters in Freemasonry*	John H. Van Gorden
18C	1987*	*George Washington in New York*	Allan Boudreau & Alexander Bleimann
19	1988	*Records of the Hole Crafte and Fellowship of Masons*	Edward Conder, Jr.
20	1989	*A Candid Disquisition of the Principles and Practices of the Most Ancient and Honourable Society of Free and Accepted Masons*	Wellins Calcott
20A	1989*	*Freemasonry and Nauvoo, 1839–1846*	Robin L. Carr
21	1990	*Masonic Odes and Poems*	Rob Morris
22	1991	*Lessing's Masonic Dialogues*	Gotthold Lessing
22A	1991*	*ABC of Freemasonry: A Book for Beginners*	Delmar D. Darrah
23	1992	*The Folger Manuscript*	S. Brent Morris
24	1993	*Freemasonry and Christianity: Lectures from Two Ages*	T. De Witt Peake & John J. Murchison
25	1994	*The Constitutions of St. John's Lodge*	Robin L. Carr
25A	1994*	*The Mystic Tie and Men of Letters*	Robin L. Carr
26	1995	*Recollections of a Masonic Veteran*	S. Brent Morris

27	1996	*The Freemason's Monitor or Illustrations of Masonry in Two Parts*	Thomas Smith Webb
28	1997	*The Masonic Ladder or the Nine Steps to Ancient Freemasonry*	John Sherer
28A	1997*	*Freemasonry and Democracy: Its Evolution in North America*	Allen E. Roberts & Wallace McLeod
29	1998	*The Masonic Harp: Collection of Masonic Odes, Hymns, Songs*	George Wingate Chase
30	1999	*Symbolic Teachings of Masonry and Its Message*	Thomas Milton Stewart
31	2000	*Freemasonry Its Meaning and Significance, An Exposition of its Ethics, Religion and Philosophy*	Otto Caspari
32	2001	*K. R. Cama Masonic Jubilee Volume*	Jivanji Jamshedji Modi
33	2002	*Caementaria Hibernica*	W. J. Chetwode Crawley
34	2003	*A Daily Advancement in Masonic Knowledge*	Wallace McLeod & S. Brent Morris
35	2004	*The Craftsman, and Templar's Textbook and, also, Melodies for the Craft*	Cornelius Moore
36	2005	*The Text Book of Freemasonry*	Retired Member of the Craft
37	2006	*Orations of the Illustrious Brother Frederick Dalcho Esq., M.D.*	Frederick Dalcho
38	2007	*Antiquities of Freemasonry Comprising Illustrations of the Five Grand Periods of Masonry from the Creation of the World to the Dedication of King Solomon's Temple*	George Oliver
39	2008	*Diogenes' Lamp or an Examination of our Present-Day Morality and Enlightenment*	Adam Weishaupt
40	2009	*Proofs of Conspiracy Against All the Governments of Europe*	John Robison
41	2010	*The Evolution of Freemasonry*	Delmar Darrah

* indicates a bonus book

The Regius Poem

The Regius Poem

THE REGIUS POEM

VOLUME ONE

of the publications
of the

MASONIC BOOK CLUB

Published by the
MASONIC BOOK CLUB
A Not-For-Profit Corporation of Illinois

Bloomington, Illinois

1970

This volume has been published

solely for the Members of the

Masonic Book Club

and is limited to

333 copies

of which this is

No. _____

© 1970, by The Masonic Book Club
Printed in the United States of America

Table of Contents

FOREWORD vii

THE REGIUS POEM, a facsimile and the Poem (as transcribed by Halliwell) 1

THE EARLY HISTORY OF FREEMASONRY IN ENGLAND,
 by James Orchard Halliwell 41

COMMENTARY ON THE POEM, by James Fairbairn Smith 43

MODERN VERSION, by Roderick H. Baxter 52

GLOSSARY, by Speth 64

Foreword

THE OLDEST EXTANT DOCUMENT in the world with direct Masonic significance is the poem known as The Regius Poem, sometimes described as the Regius Manuscript or the Halliwell Manuscript. It is believed to have been written around the year 1390; and as indicated in line 143 of the Poem itself, it is believed to have been copied from an older document. The title "Regius" attached to the document is the result of the fact that it was part of the Royal Library commenced by Henry VII and which was presented to the British Museum by George II in the year 1757.

The book is four by five and one-half inches, and is written on thirty-three folios of vellum. It was bound for George II in 1757, before presentation to the Museum. It was rebound in its present form in 1838, probably after Halliwell's discovery of its unique importance. The item was buried in the archives of the British Museum under the title "A Poem of Moral Duties" and was unknown to Freemasons for its Masonic connotations until it was discovered by James O. Halliwell, a non-Mason, in the year 1838. James O. Halliwell-Phillips (he added the name "Phillips" in 1872), was an English antiquarian, librarian and Shakespearean scholar. For years, as librarian of Jesus College, Cambridge University, he concentrated on the writings of Camden, Percy, and Shakespeare, and collected many of their works. Some of his literary works were:—Nursery Rhymes of England; Dictionary of Archaic and Provincial Words; and Outlines of the Life of Shakespeare.

The Regius Poem at one time apparently belonged to a John Thomas, since he had his name written in it twice. It apparently came out of Gloucestershire, through Ann Hart Theyer, the grandmother of the first known owner of record, John Theyer, an antiquarian, who died in 1673. After his death, his library was offered to Bodley Library at Oxford, but although Bodley's librarian, Edward Barnard, went to see the Theyer Library, and even went so far as to catalogue it, (The Regius Poem being No. 146 in his inventory), Oxford University did not purchase the Theyer collection.

The collection was then sold to Robert Scott, a London book dealer, who again had it catalogued and evaluated by two distinguished clergymen before its sale to Charles II sometime subsequent to 1678, the date of their catalogue. In that catalogue it was valued at two shillings.

The Regius Poem was listed by Bernard as "Verses of Morality, in English /entitled Institutiones Geometriae/ Secondum Euclidem." Scott's catalogue calls it "Art of Geometry in Old Verse". After its purchase by King Charles II, the Theyer collection became a part of the Royal Library. The book remained in the possession of the succeeding British monarchs until 1757, when George II gave his collection of books to the British Museum, in whose honor the collection is known as the Regius Collection.

Halliwell was the first to discover the true nature of the book. On April 18, 1839, he read a paper before the Society of Antiquarians. A portion of the paper was published in Archaeologia, for 1840, page 444. Later that year the entire talk was published in booklet form by Halliwell; the contents of this booklet is reproduced herein. Since Halliwell's discovery, this volume has been the most priceless of all Masonic treasures.

Following the 1840 reprint of the Poem by Halliwell, it has been reproduced several times, but copies, and particularly facsimile copies, are rare. An English-German reprint appeared in Hamburg, Germany, in 1842. Halliwell's "Early History of Freemasonry in England" was reissued in Second Edition form in 1843.

In 1889 H. J. Whymper had some magnificent facsimile plates produced. He printed a truly limited edition of six copies on vellum, which he presented to (i) the Prince of Wales, the then reigning Grand Master; (ii) the Duke of Connaught, who became Grand Master in 1901; (iii) he kept for himself; (iv) William J. Hughan; (v) Robert Freke Gould; and (vi) G. W. Speth. At the same time Whymper placed the plates at the disposal of Quatuor Coronati Lodge No. 2076, who used them in Quatuor Coronati Antigrapha, issued in 1889, and again in 1891. These volumes are likewise very rare.

In 1914, the Lodge of Research, No. 2429, Leicester, published a reprint by R. H. Baxter, whose modern translation has been used in this volume. Baxter's translation was also used in various editions of Mackey's Encyclopedia of Freemasonry. In 1952 the Research Lodge of Oregon published a facsimile, and a new translation by John J. Church. In 1951 and again in 1959, the Masonic Service Association reprinted the Poem in the Baxter translation.

When the Masonic Book Club was first considered, no other volume seemed as appropriate for its first selection as The Regius Poem. The help of Brother Harry Carr, Secretary of Quatuor Coronati Lodge No. 2076 was requested, and unstintingly given. Through his good offices new plates of the Whymper facsimile, the finest of all, were made by the firm of Craske, Vaus and Crampton, Ltd., of London. These were then entrusted to one of America's great printing shops, the Pantagraph Printing and Stationery Company, in Bloomington, Illinois, operated by a Masonic family, Alonzo Dolan at the turn of the century, continued through his sons, Ned and Fred Dolan, and now run by the third generation of Masons, Fred and Alonzo Dolan. For many decades this firm has printed the annual proceedings of the Grand

Lodge of Illinois and of the Supreme Council, Ancient Accepted Scottish Rite, N.M.J.

In addition to our tremendous debt to Harry Carr, we also are heavily indebted to James Fairbairn Smith of Detroit, for his splendid Commentary, and to those deceased brethren of past years, G. W. Speth, and Roderick H. Baxter. But most of all are we indebted to that unknown Operative Mason of 1390, who set down his thoughts and copied the thoughts of others, in the stirring "Regius Poem".

Louis L. Williams
Alphonse Cerza

FACSIMILE PAGES
Copied From Plates Made Of
QUATUOR CORONATI ANTIGRAPHA

*Hic incipiunt constituciones artis gemetriæ
secundum Euclydem.*

Whose wol bothe wel rede and loke,
He may fynde wryte yn olde boke
Of grete lordys, and eke ladyysse,
That hade mony chyldryn y-fere, y-wisse;
And hade no rentys to fynde hem wyth,
Nowther yn towne, ny felde, ny fryth:
A cownsel togeder they cowthe hem take,
To ordeyne for these chyldryn sake,
How they myȝth best lede here lyfe
Withoute gret desese, care, and stryfe; 10
And most for the multytude that was comynge
Of here chyldryn after here zyndynge.
(They) sende thenne after grete clerkys,
To techyn hem thenne gode werkys;
And pray we hem, for our Lordys sake,
To oure chyldryn sum werke to make,
That they myȝth gete here lyvynge therby,
Bothe wel and onestlyche, ful sycurly.
Yn that tyme, throȝgh good gemetry,
Thys onest craft of good masonry   20
Wes ordeynt and made yn thys manere,
Y-cownterfetyd of thys clerkys y-fere;
At these lordys prayers they cownterfetyd gemetry,
And ȝaf hyt the name of masonry,
For the moste oneste craft of alle.
These lordys chyldryn therto dede falle,
To lurne of hym the craft of gemetry,
The wheche he made ful curysly;

Throgh fadrys prayers and modrys also,
Thys onest craft he putte hem to. 30
He that lernede best, and were of onesté,
And passud hys felows yn curysté;
ʒef yn that craft he dede hym passe,
He schulde have more worschepe then the lasse.
Thys grete clerkys name wes clept Euclyde,
Hys name hyt spradde ful wondur wyde.
ʒet thys grete clerke more ordeynt he
To hym that was herre yn thys degré,
That he schulde teche the symplyst of (wytte)
Yn that onest craft to be parfytte; 40
And so uchon schulle techyn othur,
And love togeder as syster and brothur.

Forthermore ʒet that ordeynt he,
Mayster y-callud so schulde he be;
So that he were most y-worschepede,
Thenne sculde he be so y-clepede:
But mason schulde never won other calle,
Withynne the craft amongus hem alle,
Ny soget, ny servand, my dere brother,
Thaʒht he be not so perfyt as ys another;
Uchon sculle calle other felows by cuthe,
For cause they come of ladyes burthe.
On thys maner, throʒ good wytte of gemetry,
Bygan furst the craft of masonry:
The clerk Euclyde on thys wyse hyt fonde,
Thys craft of gemetry yn Egypte londe.

[2]

Yn Egypte he tawȝhte hyt ful wyde,
Yn dyvers londe on every syde;
Mony erys afterwarde, y understonde,
ȝer that the craft com ynto thys londe.
Thys craft com ynto Englond, as y ȝow say,
Yn tyme of good kynge Adelstonus day;
He made tho bothe halle and eke bowre,
And hye templus of gret honowre,
To sportyn hym yn bothe day and nyȝth,
An to worschepe hys God with alle hys myȝth.
Thys goode lorde loved thys craft ful wel,
And purposud to strenthyn hyt every del,
For dyvers defawtys that yn the craft he fonde;
He sende aboute ynto the londe

After alle the masonus of the crafte,
To come to hym ful evene straȝte,
For to amende these defautys alle
By good consel, ȝef hyt myȝth falle.
A semblé thenne he cowthe let make
Of dyvers lordis, yn here state,-
Dukys, erlys, and barnes also,
Knyȝthys, sqwyers, and mony mo,
And the grete burges of that syté,
They were ther alle yn here degré;
These were ther uchon algate,
To ordeyne for these masonus astate.
Ther they sowȝton by here wytte,
How they myȝthyn governe hytte:

Fyftene artyculus they ther sowȝton,
And fyftene poyntys ther they wroȝton.

Hic incipit articulus primus.

The furste artycul of thys gemetry:—
The mayster mason moste be ful securly
Bothe stedefast, trusty, and trwe,
Hyt schal hym never thenne arewe: 90
And pay thy felows after the coste,
As vytaylys goth thenne, wel thou woste;
And pay them trwly, apon thy fay,
What that they deserven may;
And to her hure take no more,
But what that they mowe serve fore;
And spare, nowther for love ny drede,
Of nowther partys to take no mede;
Of lord ny felow, whether he be,
Of hem thou take no maner of fe;   100
And as a jugge stonde upryȝth,
And thenne thou dost to bothe good ryȝth;
And trwly do thys wherseuer thou gost,
Thy worschep, thy profyt, hyt schal be most.

Articulus secundus.

The secunde artycul of good masonry,
As ȝe mowe hyt here hyr specyaly,
That every mayster, that ys a mason,
Most ben at the generale congregacyon,
So that he hyt resonably y-tolde
Where that the semblé schal be holde;

[4]

And to that semblé he most nede gon,
But he have a resenabul skwsacyon,
Or but he be unbuxom to that craft,
Or with falssehed ys over-raft,
Or ellus sekenes hath hym so stronge,
That he may not come hem amonge;
That ys a skwsacyon, good and abulle,
To that semblé withoute fabulle.

Articulus tercius.

The thrydde artycul for sothe hyt ysse,
That the mayster take to no prentysse,   120
But he have good seuerans to dwelle
Seven ȝer with hym, as y ȝow telle,
Hys craft to lurne, that ys profytable;

Withynne lasse he may not ben able
To lordys profyt, ny to his owne,
As ȝe mowe knowe by good resowne.

Articulus quartus.

The fowrthe artycul thys moste be,
That the mayster hym wel be-se,
That he no bondemon prentys make,
Ny for no covetyse do hym take;   130
For the lord that he ys bonde to,
May fache the prentes whersever he go.
Ȝef yn the logge he were y-take,
Muche desese hyt myȝth ther make,
And suche case hyt myȝth befalle,
That hyt myȝth greve summe or alle.

[5]

For alle the masonus that ben there
Wol stonde togedur hol y-fere.
ʒef suche won yn that craft schulde dwelle,
Of dyvers desesys ʒe myʒth telle: 140
For more zese thenne, and of honesté,
Take a prentes of herre degré.
By olde tyme wryten y fynde
That the prentes schulde be of gentyl kynde;
And so sumtyme grete lordys blod
Toke thys gemetry, that ys ful good.

      Articulus quintus.

The fyfthe artycul ys swythe good,
So that the prentes be of lawful blod;
The mayster schal not, for no vantage,
Make no prentes that ys outrage;   150
Hyt ys to mene, as ʒe mowe here,
That he have hys lymes hole alle y-fere;
To the craft hyt were gret schame,
To make an halt mon and a lame,
For an unperfyt mon of suche blod
Schulde do the craft but lytul good.
Thus ʒe mowe knowe everychon,
The craft wolde have a myʒhty mon;
A maymed mon he hath no myʒht,
ʒe mowe hyt knowe long ʒer nyʒht.   160

      Articulus sextus.

The syxte artycul ʒe mowe not mysse,

That the mayster do the lord no pregedysse,
To take of the lord, for hyse prentyse,
Also muche as hys felows don, yn alle vyse.
For yn that craft they ben ful perfyt,
So ys not he, ȝe mowe sen hyt.
Also hyt were aȝeynus good reson,
To take hys hure, as hys felows don.
Thys same artycul, yn thys casse,
Juggythe the prentes to take lasse   170
Thenne hys felows, that ben ful perfyt.
Yn dyvers maters, conne qwyte hyt,
The mayster may his prentes so enforme,
That hys hure may crese ful ȝurne,
And, ȝer hys terme come to an ende,
Hys hure may ful wel amende.

Articulus septimus.

The seventhe artycul that ys now here,
Ful wel wol telle ȝow, alle y-fere,
That no mayster, for favour ny drede,
Schal no thef nowther clothe ny fede.   180
Theves he schal herberon never won,
Ny hym that hath y-quellude a mon,
Ny thylke that hath a febul name,
Lest hyt wolde turne the craft to schame.

Articulus octavus.

The eghte artycul schewet ȝow so,

That the mayster may hyt wel do,
ȝef that he have any mon of crafte,
And be not also perfyt as he auȝte,
He may hym change sone anon,
And take for hym a perfytur mon. 130
Suche a mon, throȝe rechelaschepe,
Myȝth do the craft schert worschepe.

Articulus nonus.

The nynthe artycul schewet ful welle,
That the mayster be both wyse and felle;
That no werke he undurtake,
But he conne bothe hyt ende and make;
And that hyt be to the lordes profyt also,
And to hys craft, wherseuer he go;
And that the grond be wel y-take,
That hyt nowther fle ny grake. 200

Articulus decimus.

The thenthe artycul ys for to knowe,
Amonge the craft, to hye and lowe,
Ther schal no mayster supplante other,
But be togeder as systur and brother,
Yn thys curyus craft, alle and som,
That longuth to a maystur mason.
Ny he schal not supplante non other mon,
That hath y-take a werke hym uppon,
Yn peyne therof that ys so stronge,

That peyseth no lasse thenne ten ponge,   210
But 3ef that he be guilty y-fonde,
That toke furst the werke on honde;
For no mon yn masonry
Schal not supplante othur securly,
But 3ef that hyt be so y-wro3th,
That hyt turne the werke to no3th;
Thenne may a mason that werk crave,
To the lordes profyt hyt for to save;
Yn suche a case but hyt do falle,
Ther schal no mason medul withalle.   220
Forsothe he that begynnyth the gronde,
And he be a mason goode and sonde,
He hath hyt sycurly yn hys mynde

To brynge the werke to ful good ende.

Articulus undecimus.

The eleventhe artycul y telle the,
That he ys bothe fayr and fre;
For he techyt, by hys my3th,
That no mason schulde worche be ny3th,
But 3ef hyt be yn practesynge of wytte,
3ef that y cowthe amende hytte.   230

Articulus duodecimus.

The twelfthe artycul ys of hye honesté
To 3every mason, whersever he be;
He schal not hys felows werk depráve,
3ef that he wol hys honesté save;
With honest wordes he hyt comende,

[9]

By the wytte that God the dede sende;
But hyt amende by al that thou may,
Bytwynne zow bothe withoute nay.

Articulus xiijus.

The threttene artycul, so God me save,
Ys, zef that the mayster a prentes have, 240
Enterlyche thenne that he hym teche,
And meserable poyntes that he hym reche,
That he the craft abelyche may conne,
Wherseuer he go undur the sonne.

Articulus xiiijus.

The fowrtene artycul, by good reson,
Scheweth the mayster how he schal don;
He schal no prentes to hym take,
But dyvers curys he have to make,
That he may, withynne hys terme,
Of hym dyvers poyntes may lurne. 250

Articulus quindecimus.

The fyftene artycul maketh an ende,
For to the mayster he ys a frende;
To lere hym so, that for no mon,
No fals mantenans he take hym apon,
Ny maynteine hys felows yn here synne,
For no good that he myzth wynne;
Ny no fals sware sofre hem to make,
For drede of here sowles sake;
Lest hyt wolde turne the craft to schame,
And hymself to mechul blame. 260

Plures Constituciones.

At thys semblé were poyntes y-ordeynt mo,
Of grete lordys and maystrys also,
That whose wol conne thys craft and com to astate,
He most love wel God, and holy churche algate,
And hys mayster also, that he ys wythe,
Whersever he go, yn fylde or frythe,
And thy felows thou love also,
For that thy craft wol that thou do.

Secundus punctus.

The secunde poynt, as y zow say,
That the mason worche apon the werk day, 270
Also trwly, as he con or may,
To deserve hys huyre for the halyday,
And trwly to labrun on hys dede,
Wel deserve to have hys mede.

Tercius punctus.

The thrydde poynt most be severele,
With the prentes knowe hyt wele,
Hys mayster conwsel he kepe and close,
And hys felows by hys goode purpose;
The prevetyse of the chamber telle he no mon,
Ny yn the logge whatsever they done; 280
Whatsever thou heryst, or syste hem do,
Telle hyt no mon, wherseyer thou go;
The conwsel of halle, and зeke of bowre,

Kepe hyt wel to gret honowre,
Lest hyt wolde torne thyself to blame,
And brynge the craft ynto gret schame.

Quartus punctus.

The fowrthe poynt techyth us alse,
That no mon to hys craft be false;
Errour he schal maynteine none
Azeynus the craft, but let hyt gone; 290
Ny no pregedysse he schal not do
To hys mayster, ny hys felows also;
And thazth the prentes be under awe,
3et he wolde have the same lawe.

Quintus punctus.

The fyfthe poynte ys, withoute nay,
That whenne the mason taketh hys pay
Of the mayster, y-ordent to hym,
Ful mekely y-take so most hyt byn;
3et most the mayster, by good resone,
Warne hem lawfully byfore none, 300
3ef he nulle okepye hem no more,
As he hath y-done ther byfore;
Azeynus thys ordyr he may not stryve,
3ef he thenke wel for to thryve.

Sextus punctus.

The syxte poynt ys ful 3ef to knowe,
Bothe to hye and eke to lowe,

For suche case hyt myȝth befalle,
Amonge the masonus, summe or alle,
Throwghe envye, or dedly hate,
Ofte aryseth ful gret debate:. 310
Thenne owyth the mason, ȝef that he may,
Putte hem bothe undur a day;
But loveday ȝet schul they make none,
Tyl that the werke day be clene a-gone;
Apon the holyday ȝe mowe wel take
Leyser y-nowȝgh loveday to make,
Lest that hyt wolde the werke day
Latte here werke for suche afray;
To suche ende thenne that ȝe hem drawe,
That they stonde wel yn Goddes lawe. 320

Septimus punctus.

The seventhe poynt he may wel mene,
Of wel longe lyf that God us lene,
As hyt dyscryeth wel opunly,
Thou schal not by thy maystres wyf ly,
Ny by thy felows, yn no maner wyse,
Lest the craft wolde the despyse;
Ny by thy felows concubyne,
No more thou woldest he dede by thyne.
The peyne thereof let hyt be ser,
That he be prentes ful seven ȝer, 330
Ȝef he forfete yn eny of hem,

So y-chasted thenne most he ben;
Ful mekele care myȝth ther begynne,
For suche a fowle dedely synne.

Octavus punctus.

The eȝhte poynt, he may be sure,
Ȝef thou hast y-taken any cure,
Under thy mayster thou be trwe,
For that poynt thou schalt never arewe;
A trwe medyater thou most nede be
To thy mayster, and thy felows fre;   340
Do trwly al . . . . that thou myȝth,
To both partyes, and that ys good ryȝth.

Nonus punctus.

The nynthe poynt we schul hym calle,
That he be stwarde of oure halle,
Ȝef that ȝe ben yn chambur y-fere,
Uchon serve other, with mylde chere;
Jentul felows, ȝe moste hyt knowe,
For to be stwardus alle o rowe,
Weke after weke withoute dowte,
Stwardus to ben so alle abowte,   350
Lovelyche to serven uchon othur,
As thawgh they were syster and brother;
Ther schal never won on other costage
Fre hymself to no vantage,
But every mon schal be lyche fre

Yn that costage, so moste hyt be;
Loke that thou pay wele every mon algate,
That thou hast y-bowzht any vytayles ate,
That no cravynge be y-mad to the,
Ny to thy felows, yn no degré,
To mon or to wommon, whether he be,
Pay hem wel and trwly, for that wol we;
Therof on thy felow trwe record thou take,
For that good pay as thou dost make;
Lest hyt wolde thy felowe schame,
And brynge thyself ynto gret blame.
Zet good acowntes he most make
Of suche godes as he hath y-take,
Of thy felows goodes that thou hast spende,
Wher, and how, and to what ende; 370
Suche acowntes thou most come to,
Whenne thy felows wollen that thou do.

Decimus punctus.

The tenthe poynt presentyeth wel god lyf,
To lyven withoute care and stryf;
For and the mason lyve amysse,
And yn hys werk be false, y-wysse,
And throwz suche a false skewysasyon
May sclawndren hys felows oute reson,
Throwz false sclawnder of suche fame

May make the craft kachone blame, 380
3ef he do the craft suche vylany,
Do hym no favour thenne securly,
Ny maynteine not hym yn wyked lyf,
Lest hyt wolde turne to care and stryf;
But 3et hym 3e schul not delayme,
But that 3e schullen hym constrayne,
For to apere whersevor 3e wylle,
Whar that 3e wolen, lowde or stylle;
To the nexte semblé 3e schul hym calle,
To apere byfore hys felows alle, 390
And but 3ef he wyl byfore hem pere,

The crafte he moste nede forswere;
He schal thenne be chasted after the lawe
That was y-fownded by olde dawe.

Punctus undecimus.

The eleventhe poynt ys of good dyscrecyoun,
As 3e mowe knowe by good resoun;
A mason, and he thys craft wel con,
That sy3th hys felow hewen on a ston,
And ys yn poynt to spylle that ston,
Amende hyt sone, 3ef that thou con, 400
And teche hym thenne hyt to amende,
That the l(ordys) werke be not y-schende,
And teche hym esely hyt to amende,

[16]

With fayre wordes, that God the hath lende;
For hys sake that sytte above,
With swete wordes noresche hym love.

Punctus duodecimus

The twelthe poynt ys of gret ryolté,
Ther as the semblé y-holde schal be,
Ther schul be maystrys and felows also,
And other grete lordes mony mo;   410
Ther schal be the scheref of that contré,
And also the meyr of that syté,
Knyʒtes and sqwyers ther schul be;
And other aldermen, as ʒe schul se;
Suche ordynance as they maken there,
They schul mayntè hyt hol y-fere
Aʒeynus that mon, whatsever he be,
That longuth to the craft bothe fayr and fre.
ʒef he any stryf aʒeynus hem make,
Ynto here warde he schal be take.   420

xiijus punctus

The threnteithe poynt ys to us ful luf,
He schal swere neveʒ to be no thef,
Ny soker hym yn hys fals craft,
For no good that he hath byraft,
And thou mowe hyt knowe or syn,
Nowther for hys good, ny for hys kyn.

xiiijus punctus

[17]

The fowrtethe poynt ys ful good lawe
To hym that wold ben under awe;
A good trwe othe he most ther swere
To hys mayster and hys felows that ben there, 430
He most be stedefast and trwe also
To alle thys ordynance, whersever he go,
And to hys lyge lord the kynge,
To be trwe to hym, over alle thynge.
And alle these poyntes hyr before
To hem thou most nede be y-swore,
And alle schul swere the same oyth
Of the masonus, ben they luf, ben they loght.
To alle these poyntes hyr byfore,
That hath ben ordeynt by ful good lore. 440
And they schul enquere every mon
On his party, as wyl as he con,
ȝef any mon mowe be y-fownde gulty
Yn any of these poyntes spesyaly;
And whad he be, let hym be sowȝht,
And to the semblé let hym be browȝht.

Quindecimus punctus.

The fyftethe poynt ys of ful good lore,
For hem that schul ben ther y-swore,
Suche ordynance at the semblé wes layd
Of grete lordes and maystres byforesayd; 450
For thylke that ben unbuxom, y-wysse,

[18]

Azeynus the ordynance that there ysse
Of these artyculus, that were y-meved there,
Of grete lordes and masonus al y-fere.
And ʒef they ben y-preved opunly
Byfore that semblé, by an by,
And for here gultes no mendys wol make,
Thenne most they nede the craft forsake;
And so masonus craft they schul refuse,
And swere hyt never more for to use.   460
But ʒef that they wol mendys make,
Aʒayn to the craft they schul never take;
And ʒef that they nul not do so,
The scheref schal come hem sone to,
And putte here bodyes yn duppe prison,
For the trespasse that they hav y-don,
And take here goodes and here cattelle
Ynto the kynges hond, every delle,
And lete hem dwelle there ful stylle,
Tyl hyt be oure lege kynges wylle.   470

Alia ordinacio artis gemetriæ.

They ordent ther a semblé to be y-holde.
Every ʒer, whersever they wolde,
To amende the defautes, ʒef any where fonde
Amonge the craft withynne the londe,
Uche ʒer or thrydde ʒer hyt schuld be holde,

Yn every place wherseuer they wolde,
Tyme and place most be ordeynt also,
Yn what place they schul semble to.
Alle the men of craft ther they most ben,
And other grete lordes, as ȝe mowe sen,   480
To mende the fautes that buth ther y-spoke,
Ȝef that eny of hem ben thenne y-broke.
Ther thy schullen ben alle y-swore,
That longuth to thys craftes lore,
To kepe these statutes everychon,
That ben y-ordeynt by kynge Aldelston;
These statutes that y haue hyr y-fonde
Y chulle they ben holde throȝh my londe,
For the worsché of my rygolté,
That y haue by my dygnyté.   490
Also at every semblé that ȝe holde,
That ȝe come to ȝowre lyge kyng bolde,
Bysechynge hym of hys hye grace,
To stonde with ȝow yn every place,
To conferme the statutes of kynge Adelston,
That he ordeydnt to thys craft by good reson.

      Ars quatuor coronatorum.
Pray we now to God almyȝht,
And to hys moder Mary bryȝht,

[20]

That we mowe keepe these artyculus here,
And these poynts wel al y-fere,   500
As dede these holy martyres fowre,
That yn thys craft were of gret honoure;
They were as gode masonus as on erthe schul go,
Gravers and ymage-makers they were also.
For they were werkemen of the beste.
The emperour hade to hem gret luste;
He wylned of hem a ymage to make,
That mowzh be worscheped for his sake;
Suche mawmetys he hade yn hys dawe,
To turne the pepul from Crystus lawe.   510

But they were stedefast yn Crystes lay,
And to here craft, withouten nay;
They loved wel God and alle hys lore,
And weren yn hys serves ever more.
Trwe men they were yn that dawe,
And lyved wel y Goddus lawe;
They thozght no mawmetys for to make,
For no good that they myzth take,
To leryn on that mawmetys for here God,
They nolde do so, thawz he were wod,   520
For they nolde not forsake here trw fay,

[21]

Ar. byleve on hys falsse lay.
The emperour let take hem sone anone,
And putte hem ynto a dep presone;
The sarre he penest hem yn that plase,
The more yoye wes to hem of Cristus grace.
Thenne when he sye no nother won,
To dethe he lette hem thenne gon,
Whose wol of here lyf ʒet mor knowe,
By the bok he may hyt schowe, 530
In the legent of scanctorum,
The names of quatuor coronatorum.

Here fest wol be, withoute nay,
After Alle Halwen the eyght day.
ʒe mow here as y do rede,
That mony ʒeres after, for gret drede
That Noees flod wes alle y-ronne,
The tower of Babyloyne was begonne,
Also playne werke of lyme and ston,
As any mon schulde loke uppon; 540
So long and brod hyt was begonne,
Seven myle the heʒghte schadweth the sonne.
Kyng Nabogodonosor let hyt make,
To gret strenthe for manus sake,

Thazgh suche a flod azayne schulde come,
Over the werke hyt schulde not nome;
For they hadde so hye pride, with stronge bost,
Alle that werke therfore was y-lost,
An angele smot hem so with dyveres speche,
That never won wyste what other schuld reche.
Mony eres after, the goode clerk Euclyde   551
Taghte the craft of gemetré wonder wyde,
So he dede that tyme other also,
Of dyvers craftes mony mo.
Throzgh hye grace of Crist yn heven,
He commensed yn the syens seven.

Gramatica ys the furste syens y-wysse,
Dialetica the secunde, so have y blysse,
Rethorica the thrydde, withoute nay,
Musica ys the fowrth, as y zow say,   560
Astromia ys the v, by my snowte,
Arsmetica the vi, withoute dowte,
Gemetria the seventhe maketh an ende,
For he ys bothe meke and hende.
Gramer forsothe ys the rote,
Whose wyl lurne on the boke;
But art passeth yn hys degré,
As the fryte doth the rote of the tre;

[23]

Rethoryk metryth with orne speche amonge,
And musyke hyt ys a swete songe;   570
Astronomy nombreth, my dere brother,
Arsmetyk scheweth won thyng that ys another,
Gemetré the seventhe syens hyt ysse,
That con deperte falshed from trewthe y-wys.
These ben the syens seven,
Whose useth hem wel, he may han heven.
Now dere chyldren, by ȝowre wytte,
Pride and covetyse that ȝe leven hytte,
And taketh hede to goode dyscrecyon,
And to good norter, whersever ȝe com.   580
Now y pray ȝow take good hede,

For thys ȝe most kenne nede,
But muche more ȝe moste wryten,
Thenne ȝe fynden hyr y-wryten.
Ȝef the fayle therto wytte,
Pray to God to sende the hytte;
For Crist hymself, he techet ous
That holy churche ys Goddes hous,
That ys y-mad for nothynge ellus
But for to pray yn, as the bok tellus;   590
Ther the pepul schal gedur ynne,
To pray and wepe for here synne.
Loke thou come not to churche late,
For to speke harlotry by the gate;

[24]

Thenne to churche when thou dost fare,
Have yn thy mynde ever mare
To worschepe thy lord God bothe day and ny3th,
With all thy wyttes, and eke thy my3th.
To the churche dore when thou dost come,
Of that holy water ther own thow nome,   600
For every drope thou feluft ther
Qvenchet a venyal o3nne, be thou ser.
But furst thou most do down thy hode,
For hyse love that dyed on the rode.
Into the churche when thou dost gon,
Pulle uppe thy herte to Crist, anon,

Uppon the rode thou loke uppe then,
And knele down fayre on bothe thy knen;
Then pray to hym oo hyr to worche,
After the lawe of holy churche,   610
For to kepe the comandementes ten,
That God 3af to alle men;
And pray to hym with mylde steven
To kepe the from the synnes seven,
That thou hyr mowe, yn thy lyve,
Kepe the wel from care and stryve,
Forthermore he grante the grace,
In heven blyose to hav a place.

[25]

In holy churche lef nyse wordes
Of lewed speche, and fowle bordes,   620
And putte away alle vanyté,
And say thy pater noster and thyn ave,
Loke also thou make no bere,
But ay to be yn thy prayere,
3ef thou wolt not thyselve pray,
Latte non other mon by no way.
In that place nowther sytte ny stonde,
But knele fayre down on the gronde,
And, when the Gospel me rede schal,

Fayre thou stonde up fro the wal,   630
And blesse the fayre, 3ef that thou conne,
When gloria tibi is begonne;
And when the gospel ys y-done,
A3ayn thou my3th knele adown;
On bothe thy knen down thou falle,
For hyse love that bow3ht us alle;
And when thou herest the belle rynge
To that holy sakerynge,
Knele 3e most, bothe 3ynge and olde,
And bothe 3or hondes fayr upholde,   642
And say thenne yn thys manere,

[26]

Fayr and softe, withoute bere;
"Jhesu Lord, welcom thou be,
Yn forme of bred, as y the se.
Now Jhesu, for thyn holy name,
Schulde me from synne and schame;
Schryff and hosel thou grant me bo,
3er that y schal hennus go,
And very contrycyon of my synne,
That y never, Lord, dye therynne;   650
And, as thou were of a mayde y-bore,
Sofre me never to be y-lore;
But when y schal hennus wende,

Grante me the blysse withoute ende;
Amen! amen! so mot hyt be!
Now, swete lady, pray for me."
Thus thou my3ht say, or sum other thynge,
When thou knelust at the sakerynge.
For covetyse after good, spare thou nought
To worschepe hym that alle hath wroght;   660
For glad may a mon that day ben,
That onus yn the day may hym sen,
Hyt ys so muche worthe, withoute nay,
The vertu therof no mon telle may;
But so meche good doth that syht,

As seynt Austyn telluth ful ryht,
That day thou syst Goddus body,
Thou schalt have these, ful securly:—
Mete and drynke at thy nede,
Non that day schal the gnede;   670
Ydul othes, an wordes bo,
God forȝeveth the also;
Sodon deth, that ylke day,
The dar not drede by no way;
Also that day, y the plyht,
Thou schalt not lese thy eye syht;
And uche fote that thou gost then,

That holy syht for to sen,
They schul be told to stonde yn stede,
When thou hast therto gret nede;   680
That messongere, the angele Gabryelle,
Wol kepe hem to the ful welle.
From thys mater now y may passe,
To telle mo medys of the masse:
To churche come ȝet, ȝef thou may,
And here thy masse uche day;
Ȝef thou mowe not come to churche,
Wher that ever thou doste worche,
When thou herest to masse knylle,

Pray to God with herte styile,
To zeve the part of that servyse,
That yn churche ther don yse.
Forthermore zet, y wol zow preche
To zowre felows, hyt for to teche,
When thou comest byfore a lorde,
Yn halle, yn bowre, or at the borde,
Hod or cappe that thou of do,
Zer thou come hym allynge to;
Twyes or thryes, withoute dowte,
To that lord thou moste lowte;
With thy ryzth kne let hyt be do,
Thyn owne worschepe thou save so.
Holde of thy cappe, and hod also,
Tyl thou have leve hyt on to do.
Al the whyle thou spokest with hym,
Fayre and lovelyche bere up thy chyn;
So, affter the norter of the boke,
Yn hys face lovely thou loke.
Fot and hond, thou kepe ful stylle
From clawynge and trypynge, ys skylle;
From spyttynge and snyftynge kepe the also,
By privy avoydans let hyt go.
And zef that thou be wyse and felle,

Thou hast gret nede to governe the welle.
Ynto the halle when thou dost wende,
Amonges the genteles, good and hende,
Presume not to hye for nothynge,
For thyn hye blod, ny thy connynge,
Nowther to sytte, ny to lene,
That ys norther good and clene.   720
Let not thy cowntenans therfore abate,
Forsothe, good norter wol save thy state.
Fader and moder, whatsever they be,
Wel ys the chyld that wel may the,
Yn halle, yn chamber, wher thou dost gon,

Gode maneres maken a mon.
To the nexte degré loke wysly,
To do hem reverans by and by;
Do hem ʒet no reverans al o-rowe,
But ʒef that thou do hem knowe.   730
To the mete when thou art y-sette,
Fayre and onestelyche thou ete hytte;
Fyrst loke that thyn honden be clene,
And that thy knyf be scharpe and kene,
And kette thy bred al at thy mete,
Ryʒth as hyt may be ther y-ete.
Ʒef thou sytte by a worththyur mon,

Then thy selven thou art won,
Sofre hym fyrst to toyche the mete,
ȝer thyself to hyt reche.   740
To the fayrest mossel thou myȝht not strike,
Thaght that thou do hyt wel lyke;
Kepe thyn hondes, fayr and wel,
From fowle smogynge of thy towel;
Theron thou schalt not thy nese snyte,
Ny at the mete thy tothe thou pyke;
To depe yn the coppe thou myȝht not synke,
Thagh thou have good wyl to drynke,
Lest thyn enyn wolde wattryn therby—

Then were hyt no curtesy.   750
Loke yn thy mowth ther be no mete,
When thou begynnyst to drynke or speke.
When thou syst any mon drynkynge,
That taketh hed to thy carpynge,
Sone anonn thou sese thy tale,
Whether he drynke wyn other ale.
Loke also thou scorne no mon,
Yn what degré thou syst hym gon;
Ny thou schalt no mon deprave,
ȝef thou wolt thy worschepe save,   760
For suche worde myȝht ther outberste,

That myȝht make the sytte yn evel reste.
Close thy honde yn thy fyste,
And kepe the wel fro "had-y-wyste."
Yn chamber, amonge the ladyes bryght,
Holde thy tonge and spende thy syght;
Lawȝe thou not with no gret cry,
Ny make no ragynge with rybody.
Play thou not but with thy peres,
Ny tel thou not al that thou heres; 710
Dyskever thou not thyn owne dede,
For no merthe, ny for no mede;
With fayr speche thou myght have thy wylle,
With hyt thou myght thy selven spylle.

When thou metyst a worthy mon,
Cappe and hod thou holle not on;
Yn churche, yn chepyns, or yn the gate,
Do hym revera(n)s after hys state.
ȝef thou gost with a worthyor mon
Then thyselven thou art won, 780
Let thy forther schulder sewe hys backe,
For that ys norter withoute lacke;
When he doth speke, holte the stylle,
When he hath don, sey for thy wylle,
Yn thy speche that thou be felle,
And what thou sayst avyse the welle;
But byref thou not hym hys tale,
Nowther at the wyn, ny at the ale.
Cryst then of hys hye grace,
ȝeve ȝow bothe wytte and space, 790
Wel thys boke to conne and rede,
Heven to have for ȝowre mede.
Amen! amen! so mot hyt be!
Say we so alle per charyté.

[32]

Urbanitatis.

Cott. MS. Caligula A II., fol. 88.

Urbanitatis.

Who so wylle of nurtur lere,
Herken to me & ȝe shalle here.
When thou comeste be fore a lorde
In halle, yn bowre, or at the borde,
Hoode or kappe thou of tho.
Ere thou come hym alle vn to,
Twyse or thryse with outen dowte
To that lorde thou moste lowte,
With thy Ryȝth kne lette hit be do,
10 Thy worshyp thou mayst saue so.
Holde of thy cappe & thy hood also
Tylle thou be byden hit on to do;
Alle the whyle thou spekest with hym,
Fayr & louely holde vp thy chynn,
So aftur the nurtur of the book
In his face louely thou loke;
Foot & hond thou kepe fulle stylle
Fro clawyng or tryppyng, hit ys skylle;
Fro spettyng & snetyng kepe the also,
20 Be priuy of voydance, & lette hit go.
And loke thou be wyse & felle,
And therto also that thow gouerne the welle.
In to the halle when thou dost wende
Amonge the genteles gode & hende,
Prece thou not vp to hyȝ for no thyng,
Nor for thy hyȝ blood, nere for thy konnyng,
Nothur to sytte, nethur to lene,
For hit ys neythur good ne clene.
Lette not thy contynaunce also abate,
30 For good nurtur wylle saue thy state;
Fadyr & modyr, what euur they be,
Welle ys the chylde that may the:
In halle, in chambur, ore where thou gon,
Nurtur & good maners maketh man.
To the nexte degre loke thou wysely
To do hem Reuerence by and by:
Do hem no Reuerens, but sette alle in Rowe
But ȝyf thou the bettur do hym knowe.

[33]

Vrbanitatis

To þe mette when þu art sette
fayre & honestly thou ete hyt
fyrste loke þt þy handes be clene
And þy knyf be sharpe & kene
And cutte þy bred & alle þy mete
Ryȝth evyn as y̛ dost hyt ete
If þu sytte be a worthyor man
Then þy self thou art on
Suffre hym fyrst to towche þe mete
Of þy self any yf gete
Do þe beste morsell þu may not stryke
Though þu neuer so wele hyt lyke
Also kepe þy hondys fayre & welle
Fro fylynge of the towell
Ther on þu shalt not þy nose wype
Noy at þy mete þy toth þu pyke
To depe þy cuppe þu may not synke
Though þu haue good wyll to drynke
Leste þy eyen water þer by
Then ys hyt no curtesy
Loke yn þy mowth be no mete
When þu be gynnyste to drynke or speke
Also when þu seste any man drynkyng
Þat taketh hed of þy karpyng
Sone anon þu sese þy tale
Whey he drynke wyne or ale
Loke also þu scorne no mon
In what degre þu se hym gon
Nor þu shalt no mon deprave
Yf þu wylt þy owen worshyp saue
For suche wordys þu myȝth out kaste
Sholde make þe to know & taste
Close þyn honde yn þy feste
And kepe þe well fram had y wyste

In chambre amonge ladyes bryȝth
Kepe þy tonge & spende þy syȝth
Lawȝe þu not wt no grette cry
Ne rage þu not wt rybaudry
Pley þu not but wt þy peres
Ne tolle þu not þt þu heres
Nor dysken oppyn others dede
For no myȝth nor for no mede
Wt fayr speche þu may haue þy deyfte
And wt þy speche þu may þe spylt
Yf þu strede a worthyer mon
Then þy self þu art on
Lette þy wyth sholde þlace hys lasse
For murt þat ys wt occasyon lasse
When he doth speke hold þe styll
When he hath don say þy wyll
Loke yn yy speche þu be sotyll
And what þu sayste auyse þe welle
And be þose þu no mon hys tale
Noy at kyrke nor at ale
Now cryste of hys grette grace
Zeue us alle both wytte & space
Well þt to knowe & take
And honour to haue for o mede
Amen Amen so mote hyt be
So say we all for charyte

Explicit titus Vrbanitatis

Urbanitatis

To the mete when thou art sette,
40 Fayre & honestly thow ete hyt:
Fyrste loke that thy handes be clene,
And that thy knyf be sharpe & kene;
And cutte thy breed & alle thy mete
Ryʒth euen as thou doste hit ete.
If thou sytte be a worthyor man
Then thy self thow art on,
Suffre hym fyrste to towche the mete
Ere thy self any ther of gete;
To the beste morselle thou may not stryke
50 Thowʒ thou neuur so welle hit lyke.
Also kepe thy hondys fayre & welle
Fro fylynge of the towelle,
Ther on thou shalt not thy nose wype;
Nothur at thy mete thy toth thou pyke;
To depe in thy cuppe thou may not synke
Thowʒ thou haue good wylle to drynke,
Leste thy eyen water there by,
Then ys hyt no curtesy.
Loke yn thy mowth be no mete
60 When thou begynneste to drynke or speke;
Also when thou sest any man drynkyng
That taketh hede of thy karpyng,
Soone a non thou sece thy tale,
Whethur he drynke wyne or Ale.
Loke also thou skorne no mon
In what the thou se hym gon; gre
Nor thou shalte no mon Repreue repraue
ʒyf thou wylt thy owen worshyp saue,
For suche wordys thou myʒth out kaste
70 Sholde make the to lyue in euelle reste;
Close thyn honde yn thy feste,
And kepe the welle from hadde-y-wyste.

In chambur among ladyes bryʒth,
Kepe thy tonge & spende thy syʒth;
Lawʒe thou not with no grette cry,
Ne Rage thou not with Rybawdry.
Pley thou not but with thy peres;
Ne telle thou not that thou heres,
          thou not
Nor dyskeuere thyn owen dede
80 For no myrth nor for no mede;
With fayr speche thou may haue thy wylle,
And with thy speche thou may the spylle.
ʒyf thou suwe a wordyer mon
Then thy self thou art on,
Lette thy Ryʒth sholdur folow his bakke,
For nurtur that ys, with owten lakke.
When he doth speke, holde the style;
When he hath don, say thy wylle;
Loke yn thy speche thou be felle,
90 And what thou sayste a vyse the welle;
And be-refe thou no mon his tale,
Nothur at wyne nere at Ale.
Now, criste of his grette grace
ʒeue vs alle bothe wytte & space
Welle this to knowe & Rede,
And heuen to haue for our mede.
Amen, Amen, so moot hit be,
So saye we alle for charyte.

Explicit Tractus Urbanitatis.

Instructions for a Parish Priest.

Cott. MS. Claudius, A. II., fol. 127.

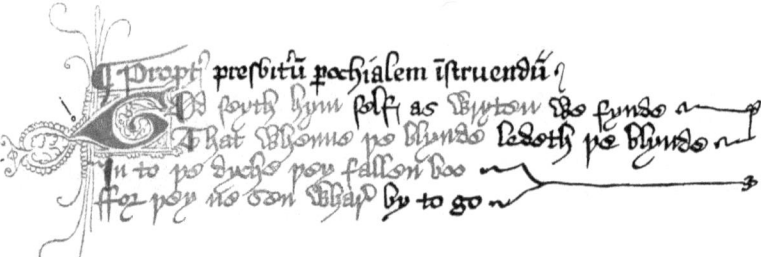

folio 130.

Зet þow moste teche hem mare
Þat whenne þey doth to chyrche fare
Þonne bydde hem leve here mony wordes
Here ydel speche and nyce bordes
And put a-way alle vanyte
And say here pater noster & here ave
No mon in chyrche stonde schal
Ny lene to pyler ny to wal
But fayre on kneus þey schulde hem sette
Knelyng doun vp on the flette
And pray to god wyth herte meke
To зeue hem grace and mercy eke
Soffere hem to make no bere
But ay to be in here prayere
And whenne þe gospelle y-red be schalle
Teche hem þonne to stonde vp alle
And blesse fayre as þey conne
Whenne gloria tibi ys by-gonne
And whenne þe gospel ys y-done
Teche hem oft to knele doune sone

[36]

Title, and first four lines of the Manuscript.

¶ *Propter presbiterum parochialem instruendum.*

God seyth hym self, as wryten we fynde,
That whenne the blynde ledeth the blynde,
In to the dyche they fallen boo,
4 For they ne sen whare by to go.

264 ȝet thow moste teche hem mare
That whenne they doth to chyrche fare,
Thenne bydde hem leue here mony wordes,
Here ydel speche, and nyce bordes,
And put a way alle vanyte,
And say here pater noster & here aue.
270 No mon in chyrche stonde schal,
Ny lene to pyler ny to wal;
But fayre on kneus they schule hem sette,
Knelynge doun vp on the flette.
And pray to god wyth herte meke
To ȝeue hem grace and mercy eke.
Soffere hem to make no bere,
But ay to be in here prayere,
And whenne the gospelle I-red be schalle,
Teche hem thenne to stonde vp alle,
280 And blesse feyre as they conne.
Whenne gloria tibi ys by-gonne,
And whenne the gospel ys I-done,
Teche hem eft to knele downe sone;

[37]

And whenne they here the belle rynge.
To that holy sakerynge.
Lokys from knelyng doune yonge & olde
And hold here hondes vp to holde
And say þenne in þys manere
ffayre and softely withouten bere.
Ihū lord welcome þou be
In forme of bred as y þe se.
Ihū for thy holy name
Schelde me to day fro synne & schame.
Schryfte & howsel lord þu grante me bo
Or that y schale hennes go.
And verre contrycyone of my synne
That y lord neuer dye ther ynne
And as þow wery of a may y bore
Sofere me neuer to be for lore.
But whenne þ^t y schale hennes wende
Grante me þe blysse withouten ende. Amen.
Teche hem þus oþer and oþer pyng.
To say at the holy sakerynge.
Teche hem also I the pray.
That whenne þey walken in þe way.
And sene þe pste a gayn hom comyng
Goddes body with hym beryng.
Thenne with gret deuocyone.
Teche hem þere to knele adoune
ffayre ne folke spare þey noghte.
To worthype hym þ^t all hath wroghte.
ffor glad may þat mon be.
þat ones in þe day may hym se.
ffor so mykyle gode doþ þat syȝt.
As seynt austyn techeth a ryȝt.
þat day þ^t þow syst goddes body.
þese benefyces schalt þ^u haue syckyrly.
Mete & drynke at thy nede.
Non schal þe þ^t day be gnede.
Idele oþes and wordes also.
God for ȝeuyþ the bo.

And whenne they here the belle rynge
To that holy sakerynge,
Teche hem knele downe bothe ȝonge & olde,
And bothe here hondes vp to holde;
And say thenne in thys manere
Feyre and softely wyth owte bere,
290 Jhesu, lord, welcome thow be,
In forme of bred as I the se;
Jhesu, for thy holy name,
Schelde me to day fro synne & schame;
Schryfte & howsele, lord, thou graunte me bo,
Er that I schale hennes go,
And verre contrycyone of my synne,
That I lord neuer dye there-Inne;
And as thow were of a may I-bore,
Sofere me neuer to be for-lore,
300 But whenne that I schale hennes wende,
Grawnte me the blysse wyth-owten ende. AMEN
Teche hem thus other sum othere thynge,
To say at the holy sakerynge.
Teche hem also, I the pray,
That whenne they walken in the way
And sene the preste a-gayn hem comynge,
Goddes body wyth hym berynge,
Thenne wyth grete deuocyone,
Teche hem there to knele a-downe;
310 Fayre ne fowle, spare they noghte
To worschype hym that alle hath wroghte;
For glad may that mon be
That ones in the day may hym se;
For so mykyle gode doth that syȝt,
(As seynt austyn techeth a ryȝt,)
That day that thow syst goddes body,
These benefyces schalt thou haue sycurly;
Mete & drynke at thy nede,
Non schal the that day be gnede;
320 Idele othes and wordes also
God for-ȝeueth the bo;

> Soden deth that ylke day,
> The dar not drede wythowte nay;
> Also that day I the plyȝte
> Thow schalt not lese thyn ye syȝte;
> And euery fote that thou goot thenne,
> That holy syȝt for to sene,
> They schule be tolde to stonde in stede
> 329 Whenne thow hast to hem nede.

Colophon to "Instructions for a Parish Priest."
(Cott. MS., Claudius, A.II., f. 152.)

> Explicit tractatus qui dicitur pars oculi de latino in angli-
> cum translatus per fratrem Iohannem myrcus canonicum regu-
> larem Monasterij de Lylleshul, cuius anime propicietur deus. Amen.

Colophon to "Liber Festivalis."
(Cott. MS., Claudius, A.II., f. 123.)

> Explicit tractus qui dicitur ffestial. Per fratrem Iohannem Mir
> kus compositus canonicum regularem Monasterij de lulshulle
> cuius anime propicietur deus. Amen.

[40]

THE EARLY HISTORY OF
FREEMASONRY IN ENGLAND

BY

JAMES ORCHARD HALLIWELL, Esq., F.R.S.,

HON. M. R. I. A., F. S. A., M. R. S. N. A., ETC.

"GOD alone is gracious and powerful! Thanks be to our gracious God, Father of heaven and of earth, and of all things that in them are, that he has vouchsafed to give power unto men!"

So commences one of the ancient constitutions of Masonry; and can we be censured for opening our task in the same spirit? An Institution which has incontrovertibly in its present form maintained a fair reputation for three centuries, is not likely to suggest any reflection worthy of condemnation. Listen, then, ye mysterious sons of Adam, to the outpourings of one who has not the felicity of numbering himself a member of your fraternity, and who has never yet had a glance beyond the confines of your mighty arcana—

> "—— more wonderful
> Than that which, by creation, first brought forth
> Light out of darkness!"

After the sun had descended down the seventh age from Adam, before the flood of Noah, there was born unto Methusael, the son of Mehujael, a man called Lamech, who took unto himself two wives; the name of the one was Adah, and the name of the other Zillah. Now Adah, his first wife, bare two sons, the one named Jabal, and the other Jubal. Jabal was the inventor of geometry, and the first who built houses of stone and timber; and Jubal was the inventor of music and of harmony. Zillah, his second wife, bare Tubalcain, the instructor of every artificer in brass and iron; and a daughter called Naamah, who was the first founder of the weaver's craft.*

All these had knowledge from above, that the Almighty would take vengeance for sin, either by fire or by water, so great was the wickedness of the world. So they reasoned among themselves how they might preserve the knowledge of the sciences they had found; and Jabal said that there were two different kinds of stones, of such virtue that one would not burn, and the other would not sink—the one called *marble*, and the other *latres*. They then agreed to write all the sciences that they had found on these two stones, Jabal having offered to accomplish this; and therefore may we say that he was the most learned in science, for he accomplished the alpha and the omega.

Water was the chosen instrument of destruction, but the two pillars of science remained in

---

* In the Charter of Freemasonry we are told, that "the seven liberal sciences are all but one science—that is to say Geometry."

triumphant security. Hermes, the son of Shem, was the fortunate discoverer of one of them. After this the craft of Masonry flourished, and Nimrod was one of the earliest and most munificent patrons of the art. Abraham, the son of Terah, was a wise man, and a great clerk, and he was skilled in all the seven sciences, and he taught the Egyptians the science of grammar. Euclid was the pupil of Abraham, and in his time the river Nile overflowed so far, that many of the dwellings of the people of Egypt were destroyed. Euclid instructed them in the art of making mighty walls and ditches to stop the progress of the water, and by geometry measured out the land, and divided it into partitions, so that each man might ascertain his own property. It was Euclid who gave Masonry the name of geometry. In his days it came to pass that the sovereign and lords of the realm had gotten many sons unlawfully by other men's wives, insomuch that the land was grievously burdened with them. A council was called, but no reasonable remedy was proposed. The king then ordered a proclamation to be made throughout his realms, that high rewards should be given to any man who would devise a proper method for maintaining the children. Euclid dispelled the difficulty. He thus addressed the king: "My noble sovereign, if I may have order and government of these lords' sons, I will teach them the seven liberal sciences, whereby they may live honestly like gentlemen, provided that you will grant me power over them by virtue of your royal commission." This request was immediately complied with, and Euclid established a Lodge of Masons.*

So far the ancient legend, which is found with occasional variations in the histories of the constitutions of Freemasonry. I have introduced it here as a preface to the very singular and curious English poem which follows, which would not be very intelligible without it.

The poem alluded to is on the constitutions of Freemasonry, and is taken from a very small quarto manuscript on vellum, written not later than the latter part of the fourteenth century, preserved in the Old Royal Library at the British Museum. (Bib. Reg. 17 A, I. ff. 32.) Casley,† by some strange oversight, in the only catalogue we at present possess, has entitled it "a poem of moral duties;" and, although he gives the Latin title correctly, yet the real contents of this singular document were quite unknown, until I pointed them out in an essay "On the Introduction of Freemasonry into England," read before the Society of Antiquaries, during the session of 1838–9. I believe I am right in stating that this is the earliest document yet brought to light connected with the progress of Freemasonry in Great Britain.

---

* MS. Harl. 1942, quoted in Freemasons' Quarterly Review, vol. iii., p. 288-295. The earliest copy I have met with is in MS., Lansd, 98, No. 48, written about 1600. Cf. the Freemasons' Magazine, Feb. 1794.

† The MS. formerly belonged to Charles Theyer, a well-known collector of the seventeenth century, and is No. 146 in his collection, as described in Bernard's *Catalogus Manuscriptorum Angliæ*, p. 200, col. 2. It was probably from this catalogue that Casley took his erroneous description, his own work being, for the most part, very carefully executed.

A POEM ON THE CRAFT OF MASONRY

Special Commentary on the Regius Manuscript

BY

J. FAIRBAIRN SMITH, F.P.S., P.M., 33°

Chairman of the Committee on Masonic
Historiology
Grand Lodge, F. & A.M. of Michigan

(AUTHOR'S NOTE: The following designations will appear in the text of this commentary: "Regius Manuscript," "Masonic Poem," "Halliwell-Phillips Manuscript," and "A Poem on the Craft of Masonry." In every instance they refer to the Regius Manuscript.)

> The Craft came into England, as I now say,
> In the time of good King Athelstan's day;
> He made them both hall and likewise bower
> And high Temples of great honor,
> To disport him in both day and night,
> And to worship his God with all his might.
> —*Lines 61 to 66 of the Poem.*

Six hundred years have elapsed since this unique and dramatically exciting Masonic Manuscript, which is today regarded as the world's oldest, was penned, and to give any commentary relative to it a startling and entirely new look is rather a frustrating and difficult project; moreover, commentaries on the Regius Manuscript have been authored during the past one hundred and thirty years by the most renowned Masonic antiquaries of the 19th and 20th centuries.

Before moving on to discuss helpful background material, we should point out that the document was probably the work of a Friar or Priest skilled as a copyist. Halliwell-Phillips, a non-Mason, is said to have discovered the Manuscript in the King's Library which was started by Henry VII and presented to the British Museum by George II. That it was a copy is intimated by Line 143, Article 4, on page xi, which says: "By old time written I find—."

Among the many 19th century antiquarians who agree that the Regius Manuscript is indeed a copy rather than original are Dr. W. Begemann of Germany and George W. Speth of England. Dr. Begemann is very positive when he says that the copyist, who may have come from a different part of the country, changed items of spelling, and he maintains that whole passages are omitted. Speth, using the same argument, declares especially that two lines are omitted between Lines 115 and 116 of the present document.

An ancient story has been told many times relating to the methods used by the Saxons to gain a foothold in Ancient Britain, which had long been tormented by the Danes and the Norsemen. The Ancient Britons, largely Celtic in origin, decided to make a treaty with the Saxons, Angles, and Jutes, commissioning them to protect the shores of the island, and the agreed-on reward was a piece of British soil which could be covered by a sheep's skin. Technically the Saxons kept their word, but by the time they were through, the hide of the sheep had been cut into a thousand pieces and spread across a large section of Britain.

A scrutiny of the development of the English language stresses that there were three distinct periods. The first begins in 450 and continues to 1150 (Battle of Hastings was fought in 1066). The characteristics of that period were: (1) An inflectional language; and (2) Use of synthetics (similar to artificial combinations used in Latin). This period is designated as Old English.

A second period in the history of the English language, beginning in 1150 and ending about 1500, shows that: (1) The language had been simplified; (2) Pronunciation of vowels had changed; (3) Inflectional qualities had been lost and endings on words had been dropped. This is the period of Middle English.

During this second period, Latin and French were spoken by the ruling classes and the clergy. English was only spoken by the common people. By 1500 English had, however, become the most important language and the changes mentioned above had been completed.

To give credence to the language claims, we find that during the period under review there are, for instance, two Latin ordinances among the Fabric Rolls of York Minster, one about 1350, the other of 1409, both near enough to the time when the Regius Manuscript had its genesis. Moreover, the trade Masons of 1356, we find, had regulations written in both Latin and French.

The third period began in 1500, when Modern English became the language of all the people. The record shows that Chaucer became the first great writer of Modern English.

Rhythm under the Anglo-Saxons during the Middle English period was always strongly marked, and we therefore find that oaths were couched in a sort of easy type of rhythm which was in use primarily to stimulate the memory and aid the ear, thus developing a rhythmic prose, flowing into irregular verse.

Perhaps the best example of this is still to be found in the old English wedding form ritual which was retained despite all the teachings and labors of St. Augustine. When the wife is taken by the man, he recites;—"to have and to hold—for better or for worse—in sickness and in health—to love and to cherish—till death us do part."

It is probable that the earliest poetry of the Anglo-Saxons consisted of single stanzas, each alluding to or narrating some exploit of a hero or God, or expressing some single sentiment; such is the poetry of early peoples. In the next stage, these stanzas were combined into connected groups and then finally the stanza arrangement was abandoned altogether.

The Regius MS. or Masonic Poem is barely carried beyond the second stage and, of course, we learn this by making a comparison with other Anglo-Saxon verse composed over a long period of time. This scrutiny demonstrates that the minstrel poets of the Saxons had by degrees composed a large mass of poetry which formed one grand and most impressive cycle. Note particularly the epic poems of Beowulf.

In order to stress the divergence of opinion which surrounds the Regius MS. we here give the reader an opportunity to scan the arguments presented by reviewers from the opposite ends of the earth whose conclusions are surely as far apart as the poles.

The first Volumes of the Proceedings of Quatuor Coronati Lodge No. 2076 of London, the world's premier research lodge, hold a veritable field day for those interested in the Regius MS. The literary giants of Masonic research of that day all made comment, and their reviews were almost as varied in point of view as there were antiquarians to write them. C. C. Howard of New Zealand in Volume IV, page 73, states: "These legends (St. Alban and Athelstan) form such an integral part of nearly all of the Old Charges that they must be a portion of the original deposit committed to the custody of English Masons . . ."

In another part of the same article, Brother Howard declares, "The Old Charges seem to be essentially English (Anglo-Saxon) documents without trace of Roman or Norman influence . . . They were Middle English in character . . . The Athelstan-Edwin legend is (with the exception of the introductory clause, linking it to the St. Alban story) a fairly accurate statement of fact that English Masonry was reorganized in the reign of King Athelstan at a meeting held at York, under the presidency of Etheling Edwin, circa 926 A.D., between that and 933 A.D."

Two years later Howard, in Volume VI, page 22, makes statements which are completely in conflict with the above conclusions. Says he: "Neither of our two oldest MSS. is a trustworthy guide in the matter of our Ancient Craft traditions. To give pride of place to the older one—the Regius MS.—we note at the outset that it is, strictly speaking, not one of the Old Charges at all, however free the use it makes of them and however close its metrical rendering of them may possibly be in certain parts . . .

"No one can read our version of the Poem through, critically, and think for one moment that it fairly represents the original sequence of thought in its author's mind. If it does, what a strangely disordered mind he must have been! But every careful reading of the MS. deepens my conviction of its Masonic untrustworthyness . . .

"The Poem as we all know divides itself into three parts:
    (a) The strictly Masonic portion
        (ll. 1–576)
    (b) A devotional manual (ll. 577–692)
    (c) A book of Etiquette (ll. 693–794)
The first is unfortunately the most imperfect. The second and third are fairly consecutive and coherent . . . Some of the Folios may have been lost, or suffered from excessive wear and tear. Others were assuredly misplaced in the copy the scribe had before him, and he was but a mechanic, too ignorant to know it or amend it."

The best known 19th century German Masonic antiquarian, Dr. William Begemann of Mecklenburg, writing in Volume V of A.Q.C., starting on page 37, simply states that he congratulates Brother Howard of the Antipodes on his indefatigable Masonic Research, but regrets that he cannot agree with him in his historic views.

Begemann declares: "Bro. Howard is of the opinion that the traditions of the Craft legend must be portions of the original deposit committed to the custody of English Masons. I do not think so, but am convinced that most of the special legends of older times as well as of the English period were introduced by degrees . . . We may learn this by comparing the different versions from the Masonic Poem down to the ordinary form.

"To begin with the introduction of Masonry into England, it is quite clear from the Poem (Regius MS.) and the Cooke MS. that only Athelstan had been connected with English Masons. There is not the least historic probability that by oral tradition any other report could have gone through so many centuries without leaving some trace in the oldest MS. Constitutions. The Poem mentions King Athelstan several times (Lines 62, 486, 595) and states in his time Masonry came into England, was favored by him with articles and points (in later times called charges) and allowed to have an Assembly every year.

"The same is told in the latter part of the Cooke MS., which is no doubt the very Old Book of Charges mentioned in former passages of this MS. I quite agree with Bro. Speth (Secretary of Q.C. 2076) who dealt with the question in his able commentary upon the Cooke MS. From this 'Old Book of Charges' and the former part of the Poem we may see at that time only Euclid and Athelstan were taken notice of in Masonic tradition.

"Now I return to the author of the Poem. After having given the Athelstan 'articles' and 'points' he adds another form of the Athelstan legend under a new title: 'Alia Ordinacio Artis Geometric,' which he has evidently taken from another source, as it differs somewhat from the former. In my opinion this 'alia ordinacio' corroborates the original absence of the Euclid legend, but in every case the repetition of Athelstan is to raise the importance of his statutes and ordinances which were to be confirmed by his successors."

Other commentaries have been made by many able writers, including Roderick H. Baxter, President of the Manchester Association of Masonic Research and Past Master of Quatuor Coronati Lodge No. 2076; John Hawkins of the Leicester Lodge of Research; and H. J. Whymper, Past Master of Quatuor Coronati Lodge No. 2076. Each has come up with conflicting opinions and divergent theories, but it can be safely said that all have made contributions and kept the wheels of thought and research working.

Any document so old is, of course, bound to excite controversy and conflicting conclusions. Opinions, no matter how divergent, are important because inevitably they lead to a solution with truth.

Although the discovery of the Regius Manuscript is credited to Mr. James O. Halliwell-Phillips, who found it in 1838, we are nevertheless reminded by Robert Freke Gould that the Manuscript was formerly in the possession of Charles Theyer, a well-known book collector of the 17th century, and it was listed as No. 146 in his library. The book is about four by five and a half inches, the writing being on a fine parchment, vellum, and is bound in a cover which bears the Royal Arms stamped on both sides, with G.R. 11 and the date 1757.

Gould also states that on the back cover are lettered the words:

POEM
ON THE
CRAFT OF
MASONRY

together with Theyer's name. The authorities at the Museum are definite about the fact that the inscription was not made at any later date, so it seems certain that the "discovery" of the oldest document relating to Freemasonry must be shared by Theyer and Halliwell-Phillips, as the former surely pointed to the nature of the contents of the volume when he lettered on the back cover his designated title and also his name.

The work is listed in Bernard's *Catalogus Manuscriptorum Angliae*, Oxford, 1697, on page 200, and is described in David Caseley's Catalogue of Manuscripts of the Old Royal Library, 1734, on page 259, as a

POEM OF
MORAL DUTIES

but its contents, because of the title, were mistaken until Halliwell-Phillips mentioned it in his paper "On the Introduction of Freemasonry to England" before the Society of Antiquaries, April 18, 1839. It was published by the author in 1840 and a second edition appeared in 1844.

Most antiquarians have placed the Regius Manuscript in the category of the Gothic Constitutions, which have also sometimes been termed York Manuscript Constitutions, since many of them declare that the first Annual Assembly of Masons was held at York. To substantiate the conclusion that at least the original of the Regius Manuscript was composed in Northumbria, Warton tells us in his History of English Poetry: "There can be no doubt that the works we possess do not fairly represent the actual literature . . . since many of the finest poems are mere fragments and those that are preserved have escaped destruction by a series of lucky chances and with a few trifling exceptions are preserved only in single manuscripts."

The reason for this statement is primarily that for some centuries after the Norman Conquest, books written in the old language were considered as waste parchment and treated accordingly; thus, great havoc was wrought among many of the great ecclesiastical libraries as a result of the Reformation.

This declaration is stressed by Maitland on page 281 of "The Dark Ages," contending that: "Whole libraries were destroyed, or made waste paper of, or consumed for the vilest uses. The splendid Abbey of Malmesbury, which possessed some of the finest manuscripts in the Kingdom, was ransacked, and its treasures either sold or burnt to serve the commonest purposes of life. An antiquary who traveled through that town, many years after the dissolution, relates that he saw broken windows patched up with remnants of the most valuable MSS., on vellum, and that the bakers had not even then consumed the stores they had accumulated to heat the ovens."

A remarkable circumstance to note is that most of the minstrels are represented to have been residents of the north of England. Most old historical songs or ballads wherein a minstrel appears characterized the eminence of the poetry as having come from "the north countrye," and indeed the prevalence of the northern dialect in a majority of compositions shows that this presentation is real.

We also learn from Warton that most of the early Anglo-Saxon poems that survived were certainly composed in Northumbria and from this he concludes "that as literature was first cultivated in the north there is *a priori* probability in the case of all of the older poems that they were either composed by Northumbrians or at least first written down in Northumbria."

In reviewing the chronology and authorship of the Regius Manuscript we can conclude that a sufficiency of evidence has been assembled to justify the strong presumption that this Masonic poem, like others of that early date, was of Northumbrian origin, and this is partially authenticated by the fact that it revolved around the narrative where King Athelstan, First King of All England, is represented as a patron and protector of the Masonic body.

Probably no historian or antiquarian has given more thought to the contents of the Regius Manuscript than Robert Freke Gould, and a rather exhaustive commentary on it was made by him and reproduced in the first volume of the Antigrapha, which is a compilation of Masonic reprints issued by Lodge Quatuor Coronati No. 2076 of London. It was printed at Margate in Keble's Gazette Office in 1889. This commentary was later made part of a volume of Masonic essays by the same author and printed in Belfast, Ireland, in 1913.

Almost all Masonic historians who have thoroughly reviewed the Regius Manuscript divide it into six divisions, but it is my opinion that the division might have been more complete if it had been extended to eight.

Division One relates the legendary history of geometry, or Masonry, and eighty-six lines are devoted to this introductory portion of the poem.

Division Two includes the fifteen articles created as a guide for the Master and the fifteen points which were set forth to rule and guide the Craftsman. This second division, in my humble opinion, should have been divided into two areas, the first to contain the fifteen articles for the Master, related in the poem by Lines 87 to 260. The second section, which expounds on the fifteen points especially prepared for the Craftsman, takes up Lines 261 to 470.

Division Three, which includes Lines 471 to 496 of the poem, relates to ordinances composed especially for Masonic assemblies. The reader, however, at this point gets the idea that both its beginning and ending are extremely abrupt, and we agree with Gould when he states that he is of the opinion that it originally came from some other legend. Certainly no adequate connection can be found between the text which precedes it or the lines which follow it. We can only conclude, therefore, that this division tells about an incomplete, fragmentary legend, badly mutilated and pitifully imperfect.

Division Four relates the legend of the Four Crowned Martyrs, which of course was never a part of English Freemasonry. It was, however, a part of the German Steinmetzen and as such was revered by the German Freemasons. This legend includes Lines 497 to 534.

The second portion of Division Four, contained in Lines 535 to 576, brings to us an even older legend of the Gild, beginning with Noah and the Flood, continuing with the Tower of Babel, Nebuchadnezzar, and Euclid, and this division of the poem ends by a presentation of the seven liberal arts and sciences.

Next we have Division Five, which is in general given over to a set of directions as to behaviour in church, and is to a great degree, perhaps, an extract from "Mirks' Instructions for Parish Priests." This division begins at Line 577 and ends at Line 692. Some authorities believe that this division has positively no relationship to Masonry, but we are inclined to think that since most Operative Masonic Lodges were attached to some ecclesiastical structure, perhaps the parish priest was not only a member of the Gild but also served as its Chaplain.

Division Six, the final portion of the Manuscript, begins at Line 693 and ends at 794, and it is almost word for word identical to "The Urbanitatis," a poem which deals in some detail with conduct at meals and also enjoins strict obedience to the habits of propriety and cleanliness and is also a guide of conduct toward all superiors.

Part Six appears to be absolutely irrelevant to the remainder of the poem. It can surely be accepted, however, as evidence that Masonry's present custom of observing gala Masonic functions by banqueting was also a feature of the Operative Craft and for this reason it is our belief that it was indeed at least a Masonic practice during the 13th and 14th centuries.

Gould states: "The plurality of legendary narrative that is met with in both exemplars (Regius and Cooke MSS.) of the group of documents, to which I have assigned the highest place as Manuscripts of the Craft, demands our attention for the following reason.

"The fact that the Manuscript Constitutions are not elsewhere referred to in any literature that has come down to us of the 14th and 15th centuries, than in the Regius and Cooke Manuscripts, is no proof that few copies were in existence at these periods."

It is also interesting to note that the designation of Regius Manuscript was pinned on the document by the same Robert Freke Gould and he did this because it came from the archives of the Kings' Library of the British Museum and because it had once belonged to a Monarch.

Many antiquarians have frowned on the idea of a Craft Gild being composed of other than Operative Masons, but the York Fabric Rolls of the 13th century make mention of many substantial men who certainly were not workmen on the Cathedral, but these men were indeed bound by ties to the Craft and were apparently accepted as such.

Thus we develop an interesting theory which reads like this:—Maybe the Regius Manuscript was the possession of a Gild and that Gild possessing it was composed of a "Speculative" or "Accepted" type of Mason. The question of such a Gild may not be a new idea, but it does excite a good deal of speculation which cannot be substantiated at this time.

The theory, however, does hold merit and

the answer might still be found in the records and Fabric Rolls of the past; for it is certain that an inner circle did exist among the skilled Craftsmen who were bonded together for long periods of time to consummate a task of great beauty and unrivalled skill.

Social psychologists down through the centuries have reflected and commented on the world and times in which they lived and operated, and an example of this is found in almost every stanza of the Regius Manuscript. This fact is established by making an analysis of the contents of the Poem.

Moreover, every passage seems to suggest a rhythmic original. It is believed that faults of construction could be placed on the compiler, but we believe in almost all cases the copyist performed honestly by rewriting manuscripts as he actually saw them.

As early as the 11th century the difference between the common language of prose and the traditional or fanciful language of poetry was distinctly felt; further, in the 12th century these differences even acted as a hindrance to the copyist who was most zealous in his efforts to preserve the original state of the document he was copying.

To go further, we find that the fifteen Articles of the Regius Manuscript are mainly imparted to us in the third person; the fifteen Points, on the other hand, are for the most part varied, but the second person appears to predominate. On reaching the Ordinances of Assembly, the copyist boldly launches forth as the direct impersonator of King Athelstan. We believe that while this is highly dramatic, it is more or less in keeping with the character of the minstrel, who might be in the habit of playing many parts and his own talent would then be able to assert itself and he would use this method to make it known to his audiences.

One thing we can safely say for the copyist is that while he probably agreed that it was a remarkable document, it nevertheless lost nothing as it was rewritten, and it is fair to assume that the imaginative story teller used his utmost skill to portray his thoughts properly, showing that he was always a philosopher and a keen observer of the scene.

As to the antiquity of the original document, it is surely evident that his frequent use of "the olde boke" should prove his desire to make it sound as though there were real antiquity behind it. We believe, however, on a closer examination, that some portions of the poem may even have been taken down from on-the-scene dictation.

Perhaps we can stress at this time that nearly a third of the poem (Lines 577-794) is plainly made up of extracts from other documents, while the Four Crowned Martyrs (Lines 497-543) are curiously wedged in without connection of any sort, which leaves some doubt as to whether they belonged in the same category. In fact, we know for certain that there is no legendary history related in the poem which would indicate that it came from a similar complete document.

With regard to the laws (Lines 87-470) we find an entirely different situation, for both the Regius and Cooke Manuscripts divide the regulations into articles and points,—a mode of arrangement which was not followed in any of the ninety-nine or more other Old Charges presently in Masonic archives. The Regius Manuscript gives fifteen of each and the Cooke Manuscript offers only eight. Perhaps this variance, coupled with the overall differences in the documents of later date, seems to warrant the assumption that several codes of laws in rhythm or meter were at some time in existence. We merely offer this information just for the sake of comparison.

Gould stated in 1882 that the Regius Manuscript displayed all the features of an epic poem rather than a simple ethical code adapted to the requirements of illiterate builders, and in 1889 he states, "A closer study of the manuscript has but strengthened this impression."

The Old Charges or Manuscript Constitutions concur with the Regius Manuscript in tracing the establishment of Masonry as a science to an Egyptian origin; they bring it into England, however, by a much more circuitous route and miss none of the classical areas of Europe. At this time York had long been regarded as the earliest legendary center of the building art. On that ancient city all trails seemed to converge, and a tradition soon grew up wherein are associated the names of King Athelstan and Prince Edwin as the patrons of Masonry.

We would like to take time out at this time to trace the line of Northumbrian Kings, but space forbids. There is no doubt about it, however, that at the age of thirty, Athelstan (925-940) succeeded his father, Edward (Ethelred), though it is doubtful that he was a natural son. In any event, Athelstan had to fight for his empire and he defeated the Kings of the Scots, the Cumbrians, and the Welsh, and these were probably the hardest battles that the Saxons had ever fought and won. He established himself at York and it is stated that during his reign he issued fourteen charters, one of which is said to have gone to Prince Edwin in behalf of the Masons of that day.

As least seven of Athelstan's grants appear to have been confirmed by every King of England from Edward the Confessor to Edward IV, and by many of them the original grantor is referred to in their charters. Of the 926 charter, however, there is not now even a single copy extant. Athelstan was succeeeded in his empire by his two younger brothers, Edmund and Edred.

Because of the success of the above mentioned wars, Athelstan's domain covered almost all of England, the southern portion of Scotland, and a small segment of Wales, and he was truly virtually King of All England.

It surely can be said that no period of Saxon history could be declared more glorious than the years of the 10th century. Unfortunately, however, the history of these fruitful years has been shamefully neglected, so little is known of the reign of the great Athelstan.

Among the seven extant charters given by Athelstan are the rhyming documents of Beverly and Ripon. These shrines were special as far as the King was concerned and he visited them frequently and handsomely endowed them. From this knowledge we generate a new thought, and since York was his headquarters, or Capitol City, so to speak, it would seem reasonable to suppose that the York Legend was in reality actual, and that he conferred the same treatment upon York as he had upon Ripon and Beverly.

One thing further comes to mind at this time. A close scrutiny of the Old Charges or Manuscript Constitutions must make us realize that when the reign of Athelstan came to an end, so did the legendary claims. In other words, the so-called "History of Masonry" as laid forth in these ancient writings has never been embellished with the record or name of another English Sovereign. From this we can conclude that York Minster is inseparably connected with the Legend of the Craft and that its origins are tied to Anglo-Saxon times.

Perhaps one other point which should be taken into consideration is the fact that the Old Charges or Manuscript Constitutions had probably become fixed or crystallized long before the Regius Manuscript took form as a writing. If we accept the credibility of this statement, we can then conclude that the legendary history and laws of the Craft were in reality copied into the latter from the former.

The above reasoning may be contrary to the thinking of most Masonic historians who believe that the separate divisions of the Regius Poem came down to us through a rhythmical channel and have, therefore, seniority over the Manuscript Constitutions, and this may well be true.

The conflict here stated should be pondered well;—we must, however, never lose sight of the fact that the York legend is only referred to by implication in the Regius Poem, whereas the Old Manuscript Constitutions positively declare the Legend of York to be part of the Ancient history of Freemasonry.

THE REGIUS MANUSCRIPT
A Poem of Moral Duties

TRANSLATION BY RODERICK H. BAXTER

Here begin the constitutions of the art
of Geometry according to Euclid.

Whoever will both well read and look
He may find written in old book
Of great lords and also ladies,
That had many children together, certainly;
And had no income to keep them with,
Neither in town nor field nor enclosed wood;
A council together they could them take,
To ordain for these children's sake,
How they might best lead their life
Without great disease, care, and strife;
And most for the multitude that was coming
Of their children after their ending.
They sent them after great clerks,
To teach them then good works;

And pray we them, for our Lord's sake.
To our children some work to make,
That they might get their living thereby,
Both well and honestly full securely.
In that time, through good geometry,
This honest craft of good masonry
Was ordained and made in this manner,
Counterfeited of these clerks together;
At these lords' prayers they counter-
              feited geometry,
And gave it the name of masonry,
For the most honest craft of all.
These lords' children thereto did fall,
To learn of him the craft of geometry,
The which he made full curiously;

Through fathers' prayers and mothers' also,
This honest craft he put them to.
He that learned best, and was of honesty,
And passed his fellows in curiosity,
If in that craft he did him pass,
He should have more worship than the less.
This great clerk's name was called Euclid,
His name it spread full wonder wide.
Yet this great clerk more ordained he
To him that was higher in this degree,
That he should teach the simplest of wit
In that honest craft to be perfect;
And so each one shall teach the other,
And love together as sister and brother.

Furthermore yet that ordained he,
Master called so should he be;
So that he were most worshipped,
Then should he be so called:
But masons should never one another call,
Within the craft amongst them all,
Neither subject nor servant, my dear brother,
Though he be not so perfect as is another;
Each shall call other fellows by friendship,
Because they come of ladies' birth.
On this manner, through good wit of geometry,
Began first the craft of masonry:
The clerk Euclid on this wise it found,
This craft of geometry in Egypt land.

In Egypt he taught it full wide,
In divers lands on every side;
Many years afterwards, I understand,

Ere that the craft came into this land.
This craft came into England, as I you say,
In time of good King Athelstane's day;
He made then both hall and even bower,
And high temples of great honour,
To disport him in both day and night,
And to worship his God with all his might.
This good lord loved this craft full well,
And purposed to strengthen it every part,
For divers faults that in the craft he found;
He sent about into the land

After all the masons of the craft,
To come to him full even straight,
For to amend these defaults all
By good counsel, if it might fall.
An assembly then he could let make
Of divers lords in their state,
Dukes, earls, and barons also,
Knights, squires and many more,
And the great burgesses of that city,
They were there all in their degree;
These were there each one always,
To ordain for these masons' estate,
There they sought by their wit,
How they might govern it:

Fifteen articles they there sought,
And fifteen points there they wrought.

    Here begins the first article.

The first article of this geometry:—
The master mason must be full securely
Both steadfast, trusty and true,
It shall him never then rue:
And pay thy fellows after the cost,
As victuals goeth then, well thou knowest;
And pay them truly, upon thy faith,
What they may deserve;
And to their hire take no more,
But what that they may serve for;
And spare neither for love nor dread,
Of neither parties to take no bribe;
Of lord nor fellow, whoever he be,
Of them thou take no manner of fee;
And as a judge stand upright,
And then thou dost to both good right;
And truly do this wheresoever thou goest,
Thy worship, thy profit, it shall be most.

    Second article.

The second article of good masonry,
As you must it here hear specially,
That every master, that is a mason,
Must be at the general congregation,
So that he it reasonably be told
Where that the assembly shall be held;

And to that assembly he must needs go,
Unless he have a reasonable excuse,
Or unless he be disobedient to that craft
Or with falsehood is overtaken,
Or else sickness hath him so strong,
That he may not come them among;
That is an excuse good and able,
To that assembly without fable.

    Third article.

The third article forsooth it is,
That the master takes to no 'prentice,
Unless he have good assurance to dwell
Seven years with him, as I you tell,
His craft to learn, that is profitable;

Within less he may not be able
To lords' profit, nor to his own
As you may know by good reason.

    Fourth article.

The fourth article this must be,
That the master him well besee,
That he no bondman 'prentice make,

Nor for no covetousness do him take;
For the lord that he is bound to,
May fetch the 'prentice wheresoever he go.
If in the lodge he were taken,
Much disease it might there make,
And such case it might befall,
That it might grieve some or all.

For all the masons that be there
Will stand together all together.
If such one in that craft should dwell,
Of divers diseases you might tell:
For more ease then, and of honesty,
Take a 'prentice of higher degree.
By old time written I find
That the 'prentice should be of gentle kind;
And so sometime, great lords' blood
Took this geometry that is full good.

Fifth article.

The fifth article is very good,
So that the 'prentice be of lawful blood;
The master shall not, for no advantage,

Make no 'prentice that is deformed;
It is to mean, as you may hear,
That he have his limbs whole all together;
To the craft it were great shame,
To make a halt man and a lame,
For an imperfect man of such blood
Should do the craft but little good.
Thus you may know every one,
The craft would have a mighty man;
A maimed man he hath no might,
You must it know long ere night.

Sixth article.

The sixth article you must not miss

That the master do the lord no prejudice,
To take the lord for his 'prentice,

As much as his fellows do, in all wise.
For in that craft they be full perfect,
So is not he, you must see it.
Also it were against good reason,
To take his hire as his fellows do.

This same article in this case,
Judgeth his 'prentice to take less
Than his fellows, that be full perfect.
In divers matters, know requite it,
The master may his 'prentice so inform,
That his hire may increase full soon,

And ere his term come to an end,
His hire may full well amend.

Seventh article.

The seventh article that is now here,
Full well will tell you all together,
That no master for favour nor dread,
Shall no thief neither clothe nor feed.
Thieves he shall harbour never one,
Nor him that hath killed a man,
Nor the same that hath a feeble name,
Lest it would turn the craft to shame.

Eighth article.

The eighth article sheweth you so,

That the master may it well do.
If that he have any man of craft,
And he be not so perfect as he ought,
He may him change soon anon,
And take for him a more perfect man.
Such a man through recklessness,
Might do the craft scant worship.

Ninth article.

The ninth article sheweth full well,
That the master be both wise and strong;

That he no work undertake,
Unless he can both it end and make;
And that it be to the lords' profit also,
And to his craft, wheresoever he go;
And that the ground be well taken,
That it neither flaw nor crack.

Tenth article.

The tenth article is for to know,
Among the craft, to high and low,
There shall no master supplant another,
But be together as sister and brother,
In this curious craft, all and some,
That belongeth to a master mason.
Nor shall he not supplant no other man,
That hath taken a work him upon,
In pain thereof that is so strong,

That weigheth no less than ten pounds,
But if that he be guilty found,
That took first the work on hand;
For no man in masonry
Shall not supplant other securely,
But if that it be so wrought,
That in turn the work to nought;
Then may a mason that work crave,
To the lords' profit for it to save
In such a case if it do fall,
There shall no mason meddle withal.
Forsooth he that beginneth the ground,
If he be a mason good and sound,
He hath it securely in his mind

To bring the work to full good end.

Eleventh article.

The eleventh article I tell thee,
That he is both fair and free;
For he teacheth, by his might,
That no mason should work by night,
But if it be in practising of wit,
If that I could amend it.

Twelfth article.

The twelfth article is of high honesty
To every mason wheresoever he be,
He shall not his fellows' work deprave,
If that he will his honesty save;
With honest words he it commend,

By the wit that God did thee send;
But it amend by all that thou may,
Between you both without doubt.

Thirteenth article.

The thirteenth article, so God me save,
Is if that the master a 'prentice have,
Entirely then that he him teach,
And measurable points that he him tell,
That he the craft ably may know,
Wheresoever he go under the sun.

Fourteenth article.

The fourteenth article by good reason,
Sheweth the master how he shall do;
He shall no 'prentice to him take,
Unless divers cares he have to make,
That he may within his term,
Of him divers points may learn.

Fifteenth article.

The fifteenth article maketh an end,
For to the master he is a friend;
To teach him so, that for no man,
No false maintenance he take him upon,
Nor maintain his fellows in their sin,
For no good that he might win;
Nor no false oath suffer him to make,
For dread of their souls' sake,

Lest it would turn the craft to shame,
And himself to very much blame.

Plural constitutions.

At this assembly were points ordained more,
Of great lords and masters also,
That who will know this craft and come to estate,
He must love well God and holy church always,
And his master also that he is with,
Wheresoever he go in field or enclosed wood,
And thy fellows thou love also,
For that thy craft will that thou do.

Second point.

The second point as I you say,
That the mason work upon the work day,
As truly as he can or may,

To deserve his hire for the holy-day,
And truly to labour on his deed,
Well deserve to have his reward.

Third point.

The third point must be severely,
With the 'prentice know it well,
His master's counsel he keep and close,
And his fellows by his good purpose;
The privities of the chamber tell he no man,
Nor in the lodge whatsoever they do;
Whatsoever thou hearest or seest them do,
Tell it no man wheresoever you go;
The counsel of hall, and even of bower,

Keep it well to great honour,
Lest it would turn thyself to blame,
And bring the craft into great shame.

Fourth point.

The fourth point teacheth us also,
That no man to his craft be false;
Error he shall maintain none
Against the craft, but let it go;
Nor no prejudice he shall not do
To his master, nor his fellow also;
And though the 'prentice be under awe,
Yet he would have the same law.

Fifth point.

The fifth point is without doubt,
That when the mason taketh his pay
Of the master, ordained to him,
Full meekly taken so must it be;
Yet must the master by good reason,
Warn him lawfully before noon,
If he will not occupy him no more,
As he hath done there before;
Against this order he may not strive,
If he think well for to thrive.

Sixth point.

The sixth point is full given to know,
Both to high and even to low,

For such case it might befall;
Among the masons some or all,
Through envy or deadly hate,
Oft ariseth full great debate.
Then ought the mason if that he may,
Put them both under a day;
But loveday yet shall they make none,
Till that the work-day be clean gone;
Upon the holy-day you must well take
Leisure enough loveday to make,
Lest that it would the work-day
Hinder their work for such a fray;
To such end then that you them draw.

That they stand well in God's law.

Seventh point.

The seventh point he may well mean,
Of well long life that God us lend,
As it descrieth well openly,
Thou shalt not by thy master's wife lie,
Nor by thy fellows', in no manner wise,
Lest the craft would thee despise;
Nor by thy fellows' concubine,
No more thou wouldst he did by thine.
The pain thereof let it be sure,
That he be 'prentice full seven year,
If he forfeit in any of them
So chastised then must he be;
Full much care might there begin,
For such a foul deadly sin.

Eighth point.

The eighth point, he may be sure,
If thou hast taken any cure,
Under thy master thou be true,
For that point thou shalt never rue;
A true mediator thou must needs be
To thy master, and thy fellows free;
Do truly all that thou might,
To both parties, and that is good right.

Ninth point.

The ninth point we shall him call,
That he be steward of our hall,
If that you be in chamber together,
Each one serve other with mild cheer;
Gentle fellows, you must it know,
For to be stewards all in turn,
Week after week without doubt,
Stewards to be so all in turn about,
Amiably to serve each one other,
As though they were sister and brother;
There shall never one another cost
Free himself to no advantage,
But every man shall be equally free
In that cost, so must it be;
Look that thou pay well every man always,
That thou hast bought any victuals eaten,
That no craving be made to thee,
Nor to thy fellows in no degree,
To man or to woman, whoever he be,
Pay them well and truly, for that will we;
Thereof on thy fellow true record thou take,
For that good pay as thou dost make,
Lest it would thy fellow shame,
And bring thyself into great blame.
Yet good accounts he must make
Of such goods as he hath taken,

Of thy fellows' goods that thou hast spent,
Where and how and to what end;
Such accounts thou must come to,
When thy fellows wish that thou do.

Tenth point.

The tenth point presenteth well good life,
To live without care and strife;
For if the mason live amiss,
And in his work be false I know,
And through such a false excuse
May slander his fellows without reason,
Through false slander of such fame
May make the craft acquire blame.
If he do the craft such villainy,
Do him no favour then securely,
Nor maintain not him in wicked life,
Lest it would turn to care and strife;
But yet him you shall not delay,
Unless that you shall him constrain,
For to appear wheresoever you will,
Where that you will, loud, or still;
To the next assembly you shall him call,
To appear before his fellows all,
And unless he will before them appear,

The craft he must need forswear;
He shall then be punished after the law
That was founded by old day.

Eleventh point.

The eleventh point is of good discretion,
As you must know by good reason;
A mason, if he this craft well know,
That seeth his fellow hew on a stone,
And is in point to spoil that stone,
Amend it soon if that thou can,
And teach him then it to amend,
That the lords' work be not spoiled,
And teach him easily it to amend,

With fair words, that God thee hath lent;
For his sake that sit above,
With sweet words nourish his love.

Twelfth point.

The twelfth point is of great royalty,
There as the assembly held shall be,
There shall be masters and fellows also,
And other great lords many more;
There shall be the sheriff of that country,
And also the mayor of that city,
Knights and squires there shall be,
And also aldermen, as you shall see;
Such ordinance as they make there,

They shall maintain it all together
Against that man, whatsoever he be,
That belongeth to the craft both fair and free.
If he any strife against them make,
Into their custody he shall be taken.

Thirteenth point.

The thirteenth point is to us full lief,
He shall swear never to be no thief,
Nor succour him in his false craft,
For no good that he hath bereft,
And thou must it know or sin,
Neither for his good, nor for his kin.

Fourteenth point.

The fourteenth point is full good law
To him that would be under awe;
A good true oath he must there swear
To his master and his fellows that be there;
He must steadfast be and true also
To all this ordinance, wheresoever he go,
And to his liege lord the king,
To be true to him over all thing.
And all these points here before
To them thou must need be sworn,
And all shall swear the same oath
Of the masons, be they lief be they loath,
To all these points here before,

That hath been ordained by full good lore.
And they shall enquire every man
Of his party, as well as he can,
If any man may be found guilty
In any of these points specially;
And who he be, let him be sought,
And to the assembly let him be brought.

Fifteenth point.

The fifteenth point is full good lore,
For them that shall be there sworn,
Such ordinance at the assembly was laid
Of great lords and masters before said;
For the same that be disobedient, I know,

Against the ordinance that there is,
Of these articles that were moved there,
Of great lords and masons all together.
And if they be proved openly
Before that assembly, by and by,
And for their guilts no amends will make,

Then must they need the craft forsake;
And no masons craft they shall refuse,
And swear it never more to use.
But if that they will amends make,
Again to the craft they shall never take;
And if that they will not do so,
The sheriff shall come them soon to,
And put their bodies in deep prison,
For the trespass that they have done,
And take their good and their cattle
Into the king's hand, every part,
And let them dwell there full still,
Till it be our liege king's will.

    Another ordinance of the art of geometry.

They ordained there an assembly to be hold,
Every year, wheresoever they would,
To amend the defaults, if any were found
Among the craft within the land;
Each year or third year it should be held,

In every place wheresoever they would;
Time and place must be ordained also,
In what place they should assemble to.
All the men of craft there they must be,
And other great lords, as you must see,
To mend the faults that he there spoken,
If that any of them be then broken.
There they shall be all sworn,
That belongeth to this craft's lore,
To keep their statutes every one
That were ordained by King Athelstane;
These statutes that I have here found

I ordain they be held through my land,
For the worship of my royalty,
That I have by my dignity.
Also at every assembly that you hold,
That you come to your liege king bold,
Beseeching him of his high grace,
To stand with you in every place,

To confirm the statutes of King Athelstane,
That he ordained to this craft by good reason.

    The art of the four crowned ones.

Pray we now to God almighty,
And to his mother Mary bright,

That we may keep these articles here,
And these points well all together,
As did these holy martyrs four,
That is this craft were of great honour;
They were as good masons as on earth shall go,
Gravers and image-makers they were also.
For they were workmen of the best,
The emperor had to them great liking;
He willed of them an image to make
That might be worshipped for his sake;
Such monuments he had in his day,
To turn the people from Christ's law.

But they were steadfast in Christ's law,
And to their craft without doubt;
They loved well God and all his lore,
And were in his service ever more.
True men they were in that day,
And lived well in God's law;
They thought no monuments for to make,
For no good that they might take,
To believe on that monument for their God,
They would not do so, though he was furious;
For they would not forsake their true faith,

And believe on his false law.
The emperor let take them soon anon,
And put them in a deep prison;
The more sorely he punished them in that place,
The more joy was to them of Christ's grace.
Then when he saw no other one,
To death he let them then go;
By the book he might it show
In the legend of holy ones,
The names of the four crowned ones.

Their feast will be without doubt,
After Hallow-e'en the eighth day.
You may hear as I do read,
That many years after, for great dread
That Noah's flood was all run,
The tower of Babylon was begun,
As plain work of lime and stone,
As any man should look upon;
So long and broad it was begun,
Seven miles the height shadoweth the sun.
King Nebuchadnezzar let it make
To great strength for man's sake,

Though such a flood again should come,
Over the work it should not take;
For they had so high pride, with strong boast,
All that work therefore was lost;
An angel smote them so with divers speech,
That never one knew what the other should tell.
Many years after, the good clerk Euclid
Taught the craft of geometry full wonder wide,
So he did that other time also,
Of divers crafts many more.
Through high grace of Christ in heaven,
He commenced in the sciences seven;

Grammar is the first science I know,
Dialect the second, so have I bliss,
Rhetoric the third without doubt,
Music is the fourth, as I you say,
Astronomy is the fifth, by my snout,
Arithmetic the sixth, without doubt,
Geometry the seventh maketh an end,
For he is both meek and courteous.
Grammar forsooth is the root,
Whoever will learn on the book;
But art passeth in his degree,
As the fruit doth the root of the tree;

Rhetoric measureth with ornate speech among,
And music it is a sweet song;

Astronomy numbereth, my dear brother,
Arithmetic sheweth one thing that is another,
Geometry the seventh science it is,
That can separate falsehood from truth, I know
These be the sciences seven,
Who useth them well he may have heaven.
Now dear children by your wit
Pride and covetousness that you leave it,
And taketh heed to good discretion,
And to good nurture, wheresoever you come.
Now I pray you take good heed,

For this you must know needs,
But much more you must know,
Than you find here written.
If thee fail therto wit,
Pray to God to send thee it;
For Christ himself, he teacheth us
That holy church is God's house,
That is made for nothing else
But for to pray in, as the book tells us;
There the people shall gather in,
To pray and weep for their sin.
Look thou come not to church late,
For to speak harlotry by the gate;

Then to church when thou dost fare,
Have in thy mind ever more
To worship thy lord God both day and night,
With all thy wits and even thy might.
To the church door when thou dost come
Of that holy water there some thou take,
For every drop thou feelest there
Quencheth a venial sin, be thou sure.
But first thou must do down thy hood,
For his love that died on the rood.
Into the church when thou dost go,
Pull up thy heart to Christ, anon;

Upon the rood thou look up then,
And kneel down fair upon thy knees,
Then pray to him so here to work,
After the law of holy church,
For to keep the commandments ten,

That God gave to all men;
And pray to him with mild voice
To keep thee from the sins seven,
That thou here may, in this life,
Keep thee well from care and strife;
Furthermore he grant thee grace,
In heaven's bliss to have a place.

In holy church leave trifling words
Of lewd speech and foul jests,
And put away all vanity,
And say thy pater noster and thine ave;
Look also that thou make no noise,
But always to be in thy prayer;
If thou wilt not thyself pray,
Hinder no other man by no way.
In that place neither sit nor stand,
But kneel fair down on the ground,
And when the Gospel me read shall,

Fairly thou stand up from the wall,
And bless the fare if that thou can,
When gloria tibi is begun;
And when the gospel is done,
Again thou might kneel down,
On both knees down thou fall,
For his love that bought us all;
And when thou hearest the bell ring
To that holy sacrament,
Kneel you must both young and old,
And both your hands fair uphold,
And say then in this manner,

Fair and soft without noise;
"Jesu Lord welcome thou be,
In form of bread as I thee see,
Now Jesu for thine holy name,
Shield me from sin and shame;
Shrift and Eucharist thou grant me both,
Ere that I shall hence go,
And very contrition for my sin,
That I never, Lord, die therein;
And as thou were of maid born,

Suffer me never to be lost;
But when I shall hence wend,

Grant me the bliss without end;
Amen! Amen! so mote it be!
Now sweet lady pray for me."
Thus thou might say, or some other thing,
When thou kneelest at the sacrament.
For covetousness after good, spare thou not
To worship him that all hath wrought;
For glad may a man that day be,
That once in the day may him see;
It is so much worth, without doubt,
The virtue thereof no man tell may;
But so much good doth that sight,

That Saint Austin telleth full right,
That day thou seest God's body,
Thou shalt have these full securely:—
Meet and drink at thy need,
None that day shalt thou lack;
Idle oaths and words both,
God forgiveth thee also;
Sudden death that same day
Thee dare not dread by no way;
Also that day, I thee plight,
Thou shalt not lose thy eye sight;
And each foot that thou goest then,

That holy sight for to see,
They shall be told to stand instead,
When thou hast thereto great need;
That messenger the angel Gabriel,
Will keep them to thee full well.
From this matter now I may pass,
To tell more benefits of the mass:
To church come yet, if thou may,
And hear the mass each day;
If thou may not come to church,
Where that ever thou dost work,
When thou hearest the mass toll,

Pray to God with heart still,
To give thy part of that service,

That in church there done is.
Furthermore yet, I will you preach
To your fellows, it for to teach,
When thou comest before a lord,
In hall, in bower, or at the board,
Hood or cap that thou off do,
Ere thou come him entirely to;
Twice or thrice, without doubt,
To that lord thou must bow;
With thy right knee let it be done,

Thine own worship thou save so.
Hold off thy cap and hood also,
Till thou have leave it on to put.
All the time thou speakest with him,
Fair and amiably hold up thy chin;
So, after the nurture of the book,
In his face kindly thou look.
Foot and hand thou keep full still,
For clawing and tripping, is skill;
From spitting and sniffling keep thee also,
By private expulsion let it go.
And if that thou be wise and discrete,

Thou has great need to govern thee well.
Into the hall when thou dost wend,
Amongst the gentles, good and courteous,
Presume not too high for nothing,
For thine high blood, nor thy cunning,
Neither to sit nor to lean,
That is nurture good and clean.
Let not thy countenance therefore abate,
Forsooth good nurture will save thy state.
Father and mother, whatsoever they be,
Well is the child that well may thee,
In hall, in chamber, where thou dost go;

Good manners make a man.
To the next degree look wisely,
To do them reverence by and by;
Do them yet no reverence all in turn,
Unless that thou do them know.
To the meat when thou art set,

Fair and honestly thou eat it;
First look that thine hands be clean,
And that thy knife be sharp and keen,
And cut thy bread all at thy meat,
Right as it may be there eaten.
If thou sit by a worthier man.

Then thy self thou art one,
Suffer him first to touch the meat,
Ere thyself to it reach.
To the fairest morsel thou might not strike,
Though that thou do it well like;
Keep thine hands fair and well,
From foul smudging of thy towel;
Thereon thou shalt not thy nose blow,
Nor at the meat thy tooth thou pick;
Too deep in cup thou might not sink,
Though thou have good will to drink,
Lest thine eyes would water thereby—

Then were it no courtesy.
Look in thy mouth there be no meat,
When thou beginnest to drink or speak.
When thou seest any man drinking,
That taketh heed to thy speech,
Soon anon thou cease thy tale,
Whether he drink wine or ale,
Look also thou scorn no man,
In what degree thou seest him gone;
Nor thou shalt no man deprave,
If thou wilt thy worship save;
For such word might there outburst.

That might make thee sit in evil rest.
Close thy hand in thy fist,
And keep thee well from "had I known."
In chamber, among the ladies bright,
Hold thy tongue and spend thy sight;
Laugh thou not with no great cry,
Nor make no lewd sport and ribaldry.
Play thou not but with thy peers,
Nor tell thou not all that thou hears;
Discover thou not thine own deed,

For no mirth, nor for no reward;
With fair speech thou might have thy will,
With it thou might thy self spoil.

When thou meetest a worthy man,
Cap and hood thou hold not on;
In church, in market, or in the gate,
Do him reverence after his state.
If thou goest with a worthier man
Then thyself thou art one,
Let thy foremost shoulder follow his back,
For that is nurture without lack;

When he doth speak, hold thee still,
When he hath done, say for thy will,
In thy speech that thou be discreet,
And what thou sayest consider thee well;
But deprive thou not him his tale,
Neither at the wine nor at the ale.
Christ then of his high grace,
Save you both wit and space,
Well this book to know and read,
Heaven to have for your reward.
Amen! Amen! so mote it be!
So say we all for charity.

A
GLOSSARY

BY

G. W. SPETH

The character "ȝ" in the Manuscript is derived from the Anglo-Saxon "g" and expresses the sounds of g and y. To facilitate reference I have, in this glossary, treated it as a 27th letter of the alphabet, placing it immediately after z.

The letters p, u, and i, prefixed to numerical figures, refer to lines in the Regius MS., Urbanitatis, and Instructions for a Parish Priest, respectively.

Abelyche	p 243, *ably*	Berefe	u 91, *bereave, deprive, cut short*
Abowte	p 350, *in turn about*		
Abulle	p 117, *able, sufficient*	Berynge	i 307, *bearing*
Acowntes	p 367, 371, *accounts, reckoning*	Be-se	p 128, *besee, observe, bear in mind*
Adown	p 634, *down*	Blod	p 145,148,155, & elsewhere *blood*
Agayn	i 306, *against, towards*		
Agone	p 314, *gone, ended*	Bo	p 647,671, i 294 & elsewhere *both*
Algate	p 81, 264, 357, *always, by all means*	Bok	p 530, 590, *book*
Allynge to	p 698, *all into, i.e. entirely*	Boke	p 2, 566, 707, & elsewhere *book*
Alse	p 287, *also*		
Also	p 164,188,271, & elsewhere *as*	Bonde	p 131, *in bondage or villeinage*
Amende	p 400, *amend, rectify*	Bondemon	p 129, *bondman, villein*
Amongus	p 48, *amongst*	Boo	i 3, *both*
A-mysse	p 375, *amiss, improperly*	Bordes	p 620, i 267, *jests*
An	p 66, 522, 671, *and*	Bost	p 547, *boast*
And	p 222, 375, 397, *if*	Bowȝht	p 636, *bought*
Anone	p 523, *anon, at once*	Browȝht	p 446, *brought*
Apere	p 387, 390, *appear*	Bryȝth	u 73, *bright*
Apon	p 93, 254, 270, & elsewhere *upon*	Burges	p 79, *burgesses*
		Burthe	p 52, *birth*
Arewe	p 90, 338, *rue, regret, repent*	But	p 112, 113, 248, 391, *unless, excepting*
Arsmetyk	p 572, *arithmetic*		
Artycul	p 87, 105, 119, & elsewhere *article*	Buth	p 481, *be-eth, i.e. are, or shall be*
Artyculus	p 85, 453, 499, & elsewhere *articles*	Bydde	i 266, *bid*
		Byden	u 12, *bidden*
Astate	p 82, 263, *estate, dignity, honour*	By-gonne	i 281, *begun*
		Byn	p 298, *be*
Aue	i 269, *ave*	Byraft	p 424, *bereft, deprived*
Auȝte	p 188, *ought*	Byref	p 787, *bereave, deprive, shorten*
Avoydans	p 712, *expulsion*		
Avyse	p 786, u 90, *avise, consider*	Bytwyune	p 238, *between*
Ay	p 624, i 277, *aye, always, ever, continually*	Carpynge	p 754, *speech* (Shakespeare uses the word for jesting)
Aȝayn	p 462, 545, 634, *again*	Casse	p 169, *case*
Aȝeynus	p 167,290,303, & elsewhere *against*	Cattelle	p 467, *chattels, goods, property*
		Chasted	p 393, *chastised, punished*
Bakke	u 85, *back*	Chepyns	p 777, *markets, cheapings,* c.f. Cheapside and East Cheap in the City of London)
Barnes	p 77, *barons*		
Ben	p 124, 448, &c., *be* (infinitive), p 137, 165, &c., *are* (3rd person plur.), p 438, &c., *be* (subjunctive)		
		Chere	p 346, *chear or cheer, entertainment*
Bere	p 623,642, i 276 & elsewhere *noise, cry*	Chulle	p 488, *will, ordain*
		Clawynge	p 710, *clawing, touching*

[65]

Clept	p 35, *called, named*	Eft	i 283, *after*
Com	p 60, 61, *came,* p 588, *come*	Eghte	p 185, 335, *eighth*
Commenced	p 556, *graduated, took a degree*	Eke	p 3,64,306,& elsewhere,*also*
		Ellus	p 115, 589, *else*
Con	p 271, 400, 442, 574, *can,* p 397, *know*	Enforme	p 174, *inform, i.e. instruct, teach*
Conne	p 172,243,263,&elsewhere *know,* p 196, 791, and elsewhere, *can*	Enquere	p 441, *inquire*
		Enterlyche	p 241, *entirely, completely, fully*
Connynge	p 718, *knowledge, skill*	Enyn	p 749, *eyes*
Consel	p 74, *counsel*	Er	i 295, *ere, before*
Conwsel	p 277, 283, *counsel*	Eres	p 551, *years*
Coppe	p 747, *cup*	Erlys	p 77, *earls*
Costage	p 353, 356, *cost, expense*	Erys	p 59, *years*
Covetyse	p 130, 578, 650, *covetousness*	Esely	p 403, *easily*
Cownterfeityd	p 23, *counterfeited, imitated*	Ete	p 732, u 40, 44, *eat*
Cowthe	p 7, 75, 230 (*couth*, Saxon, to know), *could, knew*	Euelle	u 70, *evil*
		Euur	u 31, *ever*
Crese	p 174, *increase*	Everychon	p 157, 485, *everyone*
Criste	u 93, *Christ*	Eyen	u 57, *eyes*
Cristus	p 526, *Christ's*	Eyght	p 534, *eighth*
Cryst	p 789, *Christ*		
Crystes	p 511, *Christ's*	Fabulle	p 118, *fable* (in the sense of falsehood)
Crystus	p 510, *Christ's*		
Curys	p 248, *cares*	Fache	p 132, *fetch*
Curysly	p 28, *curiously, i.e. carefully, nicely*	Fader	p 723, *father*
		Fadrys	p 29, *fathers'*
Curysté	p 32, *curiosity, i.e. nicety, accuracy, skill*	Fadyr	u 31, *father*
		Falle	p 74, 219, *befall, happen*
Curyus	p 205, *curious, i.e. nice, ingenious*	Fare	p 595, i 265, *go*
		Fautes	p 481, *faults, defects*
Cuthe	p 51, *friendship* (*cuth* in Saxon, *known*)	Fay	p 93, 521, *faith*
		Fayr	p 226,418,640,&elsewhere *fair, fairly, well*
Dawe	p 394, 509, 515, *day, days*	Fayre	p 608,628 631,&elsewhere *fairly*
Dede	p 20, 32, 236 & elsewhere, *did*		
		Fe	p 100, *fee* (in the sense of a bribe)
Dede	p 275, 771, *deed*		
Dedely	p 334, *deadly*	Febul	p 183, *feeble, week, poor*
Defautes	p 473, *defects*	Felde	p 6, *field, plain*
Defautys	p 73, *defects*	Felle	p 194,713,785,&elsewhere *strong, stern, discreet*
Defawtys	p 69, *defects*		
Del	p 68, *part, portion,* (akin to *deal* and *dole*)	Felust	p 601, *feelest*
		Fest	p 533, *feast, festival*
Delayme	p 385, *delay, i.e. hinder in his work*	Feste	u 71, *fist*
		Feyre	i 280, 289, *fairly*
Delle	p 468, *part,* (see Del)	Fle	p 200, *fly, flaw*
Dep	p 524, *deep*	Flette	i 273, *flat, flagstone*
Deperte	p 574, *depart, separate*	Fonde	p 69, 473, *found, discovered*
Deserven	p 94, *deserve* (plur.)	Fonde	p 56, *founded, established*
Desese	p 10, 134, *dis-ease, uneasiness, trouble*	For	p 784, *forth*
		Forfete	p 331, *forfeit, offend, beguilty*
Desesys	p 140, *troubles*	Forlor	i 299, *forlorn, forsaken, lost*
Deuocyone	i 308, *devotion*	Forther	p 781, *formost*
Do	p 701, *done*	For-ȝeuth	i 321, *forgiveth*
Don	p 164,168,246,&elsewhere *do*	Fot	p 709, *foot*
		Fote	p 677, i 326, *foot*
Don	p 784, u 88, *done*	Fowle	p 620, *foul, lewd,* p 744, *dirty*
Dowte	p 562, u 7, *doubt*		
Drede	p 97,179, 258, & elsewhere *dread, fear*	Fowre	p 501, *four*
		Fowrtethe	p 427, *fourteenth*
Duppe	p 465, *deep*	Fowrthe	p 127, 287, *fourth*
Dyche	i 3, *ditch*	Fre	p 226,340,355,&elsewhere *free*
Dyscryeth	p 323, *decrieth, forbids*		
Dyskeuere	u 79, *discover, made known*	Fro	p 630, 764, u 52, & elsewhere, *from*
Dyskever	p 771, *discover, made known*		

[66]

Fryte	p 568, *fruit*	Honden	p 733, } *hands*
Fryth, Frythe	p 6, 266, *an enclosed wood*	Houdys	u 51, }
Fylde	p 266, *field*	Honowre	p 64, *honour*
Fyftethe	p 447, *fifteenth*	Hosel	p 647, } *the Eucharist,*
Fylynge	u 52, *defiling, soiling, dirtying*	Howsele	i 294, } *Lord's Supper*
Fynde	p 5, *find, provide for*	Hure	p 95, 168, 175, &c. } *hire, pay,*
Fynden	p 684, *find* (plur.)	Huyre	p 272, } *wages*
Gedur	p 591, *gather, assemble*	Hye	p 64, 202, 231, & elsewhere *high*
Gemetry	p 19, 24, 27, & elsewhere, *geometry*	Hyr	p 106, & elsewhere, *hear*
Gentul	p 347, *gentle, well-born*	Hyr	p 435, 439, 487, &c., *here*
Gentyl	p 144, *gentle*	Hyse	p 163, 604, 636, *his*
Gete	u 48, *get, gettest*	Hyt	p 25, 36, 55, &c., } *it*
Gnede	p 670, 1319, *wanting, lacking*	Hytte	p 84, 230, 586, &c., }
God	p 373, *good*	Hyʒ	u 25, 26, *high*
Goddus	p 516, 667, *God's*		
Gode	p 14, 503, 726, & elsewhere *good*	I-bore	i 298, *born*
		Idele	i 320, *idle*
Godes	p 368, *goods*	I-done	i 282, *done*
Gon	p 111, 290, 528, *go*	I-red	i 278, *read*
Gost	p 103, 677, 779, & elsewhere *goest*	Jugge	p 101, *judge*
Goth	p 92, *go*	Juggythe	p 170, *judgeth, adjudgeth, decrees*
Grake	p 200, *crack*		
Gravers	p 504, *engravers*		
Grawnte	i 301, *grant*	Kachone	p 380, *catch, acquire*
Grete	p 3, 13, & elsewhere, *great*	Karpynge	u 62, *speech*
Greve	p 136, *grieve, offend*	Kenne	p 582, *know*
Gronde	p 199, 221, 628, *ground, foundation*	Kette	p 735, *cut*
		Knelust	p 658, *kneelest*
Gultes	p 457, *guilt, faults*	Knen	p 608, 635, } *knees*
		Kneus	i 272 }
Had-y-wyste	p 764, } *Had I known, an expression of unavailing regret*	Knylle	p 689, *knell, toll, ring*
		Knyʒtes	p 413, } *knights*
Hadde-y-wyste	u 72, }	Knyʒthys	p 78, }
Halwen	p 534, *Hallow e'en, All Saints'*	Kunnyng	u 26, *cunning, i.e. knowledge, skill*
Han	p 576, *to have*	Kynde	p 144, *kin, lineage*
Hed	p 754, } *heed, attention*	Labrun	p 273, *to labour, work*
Hede	u 62, }	Lacke	p 782, *lack, blame*
Hem	p 5, 7, 14, and elsewhere, *them*	Ladyysse	p 3, *ladies*
		Lakke	u 86, *lack, stint, blame*
Hende	p 564, 716, u 24, *courteous, civil, gentle*	Lame	p 378, *often*
		Lasse	p 34, 124, 170, 210, *less*
Hennes	i 295, 300, } *hence*	Latte	p 318, 626, *let, hinder*
Hennus	p 648, 653, }	Lawe	p 510, 516, *law*
Her	p 95, *their*	Lawʒe	p 767, u 75, *laugh*
Herberon	p 181, *harbour, protect*	Lay	p 511, 522, *law*
Here	p 9, 12, 17, and elsewhere, *their*	Lede	p 9, *lead*
		Lef	p 619, *leave, desist from*
Here	p 535, 616, u 2, & elsewhere *hear*	Lege	p 470, *liege*
		Lende	p 404, *lent, given*
Heres	p 770, u 78, *hearest*	Lene	p 322, *lend, grant*
Herre	p 38, 142, *higher*	Lere	p 253, u 1, *learn, teach*
Heryst	p 281, *hearest*	Lernede	p 31, *learnt*
Hewen	p 398, *to hew*	Lese	p 676, i 325, *lose*
Heʒghte	p 542, *height*	Lete	p 469, *let*
Hit	u 9, 12, *it*	Leyser	p 316, *leisure*
Hod	p 697, 703, 776, } *hood*	Leven	p 578, *leave, abandon*
Hode	p 603, }	Levyn	p 519, *believe*
Hol	p 138, 416, *all*	Logge	p 133, 280, *lodge*
Holde	p 110, 475, 483, *holden, held*	Loght	p 438, *loath*
Hole	p 152, *whole*	Loke	p 1, 357, 540, &c., *look*
Holle	p 776, } *hold, keep*	Londe	p 56, 58, 60, & elsewhere, *land, country*
Holte	p 783, }		
Hond	p 468, 709, } *hand*	Longuth	p 206, 418, 484, *belongeth, beseemeth*
Honde	p 212, 640, 763, }		

[67]

Loveday	p 313, 316, *a day set apart for the friendly adjustment of differences*	Mow Mowe Mowȝh	p 535, p 96, 106, &c. } *may* p 508, *might*
Lovelyche	p 351, 706, *lovely, amiably*	My	p 49, *but* (compare *mais*, French; *ma*, Italian)
Lowte	p 700, u 86, *bow*		
Luf	p 421, 438, *lief, dear, willing*	Mykyle	i 314, *much*
Luste	p 506, *liking*	Mysse	p 161, *miss, evade*
Lyche	p 355, *like, alike, equally*	Mytȝth	p 74,
Lyf	p 373, 383, *life*	Myȝght	p 747, } *might*
Lyge	p 433, 492, *liege*	Myȝth	p 9, 17, &c.
Lȳmes	p 152, *limbs*	Myȝthyn	p 84, *might* (plur.)
Lytul	p 156, *little*		
Lyven	p 374, *to live*	Name	p 183, *repute, reputation*
		Ne	u 28, 76, 78, i 4, *nor*
Maken	p 415, 726, *make* (plur.)	Nede	p 111, 339, 392, & elsewhere *needs, of necessity*
Manere	p 21, *manner*		
Mantenans	p 254, *maintenance*	Nere	u 26, 92, *nor*
Mare	p 596, i 264, *more*	Nese	p 745, *nose*
Masonus	p 438, 454, 459, & elsewhere *mason's*	Nethur	u 27, *nor*
		Neuur	u 50, *never*
Maters	p 172, *matters*	Neythur	u 28, *neither*
Mawmetys	p 509, 517, 519, *idols* (this word is corrupted from Mahomet)	Noees	p 537, *Noah's*
		Noghte	u 310, *naught, nought*
		Nolde	p 520, 521, *would not*
May	i 298, *maid*	Nome	p 546, 600, *take*
Mayde	p 651, *maid*	Non	p 207, 626, 670, *no, none*
Maynte	p 416,	None	p 300, *nones, the 9th hour of the day, 3 p.m.*
Maynteine	p 255, 289, 383, } *maintain*		
Mayster	p 44, 88, 107, & elsewhere *master*	Noresche	p 406, *nourish*
		Norter	p 580, 707, 782, & elsewhere *nurture*
Maystres	p 324, *master's*, p 450, *masters*		
Maystrys	p 262, 409, *masters*	Norther	p 720, *nurture*
Meche	p 665, } *much*	Nother	p 527, *other* (with the negative participle)
Mechul	p 260,		
Mede	p 98, 274, 772, & elsewhere *reward, bribe*	Nothur	u 27, 54, 92, } *neither*
		Nowther	p 6, 97, 98, &c.
Medul	p 220, *meddle*	Noȝth	p 216, *nought*
Medys	p 684, *rewards, benefits*	Nul	p 463, } *will* (used negatively with no or not)
Meke	p 564, *meek, lowly*		
Mekele	p 333, *mickle, much*	Nulle	p 301,
Mekely	p 298, *meekly, i.e. without complaint*	Nurtur	u 1, 15, 30, and elsewhere, *nurture*
Mene	p 151, 321, *mean, signify, say*	Ny	p 6, 49, 97, & elsewhere, *nor*
Mendys	p 457, 461, *amends*	Nyce	i 267, } *nice, foppish, vain, trifling*
Merthe	p 772, *mirth*	Nyse	p 19,
Meserable	p 242, *measurable*	Nyȝth	p 65, 228, 597, *night*
Metryth	p 569, *measureth*		
Metyst	p 775, *meetest*	Of	p 697, 703, u 5, 11, *off*
Meyr	p 412, *mayor*	Ogth	p 437, *oath*
Mo	p 78, 261, 410, & elsewhere *more*	Okepye	p 301, *occupy*
		On	u 46, 84, *one*
Moder	p 498, 723, *mother*	Ones	i 313, *once*
Modrys	p 29, *mother's*	Onest	p 20, 30, 40, } *honest, honourable*
Modyr	u 31, *mother*	Oneste	p 25,
Mon	p 154, 155, 158, & elsewhere *man*	Onesté	p 31, *honesty*
		Onestlyche	p 18, 732, *honestly*
Monus	p 554, *man's*	Onus	p 660, *once*
Mony	p 59, 78, 410, & elsewhere *many*	Ordent	p 471, } *ordained*
		Ordeydnt	p 496,
Moot	u 97, *mote, might, let*	Ordeynt	p 21, 37, 43, &c.
Mossel	p 741, *morsel*	Ordyr	p 303, *order, ordinance*
Most	p 11, *mostly, chiefly*	Orne	p 569, *ornate, adorned*
Most	p 108, 111, 264, & elsewhere } *must*	O-rowe	p 348, 729, *in a row, in turn, one after the other*
Moste	p 88, 127, 347, & elsewhere	Othe	p 429, i 320, *oath*
		Other	p 756, i 302, *or*
Mot	p 655, 793, *mote, might, let*	Ous	p 587, *us*

Oute	p 378, *without*	Sarro	p 525, *more sorely*
Outrage	p 150, *deformed*	Say	p 269, 560, *tell*
Over	p 434, *above*	Schadweth	p 542, *shadoweth*
Over-raft	p 114, *over-reft, over-taken, convicted*	Schal	p 90, 104, 110, &c. ⎫
		Schalo	i 295, 300 ⎬ *shall*
Owen	u 68, 79, *own*	Schalle	i 278 ⎭
Owte	i 289, ⎫ *out*	Schame	p 259, 286, &c., *shame*
Owten	u 86, i 301, ⎭	Schelde	i 293, *shield*
		Schsref	p 411, 464, *sheriff*
Parfytte	p 40, *perfect*	Schert	p 192, *short, scant*
Passud	p 32, *passed, surpassed, excelled*	Schowet	p 185, 193, *showeth*
		Schryff	p 647, ⎫ *shrift, confession*
Penest	p 525, *punished, pained*	Schryfte	i 294, ⎭
Pepul	p 510, 591, *people*	Schul	p 313, 385, 389, &c., *shall*
Pere	p 391, *appear*	Schulde	p 39, 44, 47, &c., *should*
Perfyt	p 50, 165, 171, & elsewhere *perfect, skilled*	Schulde	p 646, *shield*
		Schulder	p 781, *shoulder*
Perfytur	p 190, *perfecter, more skilled*	Schule	i 272, 328, ⎫ *shall*
Peyne	p 209, 329, *pain, penalty*	Schulle	p 41, ⎭
Peyseth	p 210, *weigheth*, (French *peser*, to weigh)	Schullen	p 386, 483, *shall* (plural)
		Sckylle	p 710, *skill*
Pley	u 77, *play, gamble*	Sclawnder	p 379, *slander*
Plyht	p 675, ⎫ *plight, promise*	Sclawndren	p 378, *to slander, disgrace*
Plyʒte	i 324, ⎭	Sculde	p 46, *should*
Ponge	p 210, *pound*	Sculle	p 51, *shall*
Poyntys	p 86, *points*	Se	p 414, 644, i 213, u 66, &c., *see*
Prece	u 25, *press*		
Pregedysse	p 162, 291, *prejudice, injury*	Sece	u 63, *cease*
Prentes	p 132, 142, &c. ⎫	Securly	p 88, 214, and elsewhere, *securely, surely*
Prentys	p 129, ⎬ *prentice,*		
Prentyse	p 163, ⎱ *apprentice*	Sekenes	p 115, *sickness*
Prentysse	p 120,	Selven	p 738, 774, *self*
Presone	p 524, *prison*	Semble	p 478, *assemble*
Prevetyse	p 270, *privities, private matters, secrets*	Semblé	p 75, 110, 111, &c., *assembly*
		Sen	p 166, 480, i 4, & elsewhere *to see, they see*
Pyler	i 271, *pillar*		
Pyke	p 746, u 54, *pick*	Sende	p 70, *sent*
		Sene	i 306, 327, *to see*
Qwenchet	p 602, *quenches*	Ser	p 329, 602, *sure*
Qwyte	p 172, *requite*	Servand	p 49, *servant*
		Serven	p 351, *serve, wait upon*
Rage	u 76, *break bounds, riot*	Serves	p 514, *service*
Ragynge	p 768, *lewd sport*, (Chaucer employs *Ragery* for *wantonness*)	Sese	p 755, *cease*
		Sest	u 61, *seest*
		Seuerans	p 121, *assurance, security*
Reche	p 242, 550, *tell*, from Sax., *reccan*, to say, tell, narrate, allied to reek, reckon, & reach)	Sewe	p 781, *follow*, (French, *suivre*)
		Sey	p 784, *say*
		Seynt	p 666, i 315, *saint*
Reeche	p 740, *reach*	Scyth	i 1, *saith, says*
Rechelaschepe	p 191, *recklessness*	Sholde	u 70, *should*
Rentys	p 5, *income*	Sholdur	u 85, *shoulder*
Repreue	u 67, *reprove*	Skewsnsyon	p 377, *excuse*
Resenabul	p 112, *reasonable*	Skwsacyon	p 112, 117, *excuse*
Resowne	p 126, *reason*	Smogynge	p 744, *smudging, soiling*
Rode	p 604, 607, *the Rood, Cross*	Snetyng	u 19, ⎫ *sniffling, snuffling,*
Rote	p 565, 568, *root*		⎬ *wiping your nose*
Rybawdry	u 68, ⎫ *ribaldry*	Sniftynge	p 711, ⎭ *with your fingers*
Rybody	p 768, ⎭	Snowte	p 561, *snout, nose*
Rygolté	p 489, *royalty*	Snyte	p 745, *to blow the nose*
Ryht	p 666, *right*	So	p 148, probably a mistake for *se*
Ryolté	p 407, *royalty*		
Ryʒt	i 315, ⎫ *right*	Soden	i 322, *sudden*
Ryʒth	p 102, 342, &c. ⎭	Sofere	i 298, ⎫ *suffer,*
		Soffere	i 276, ⎬ *permit*
Sakerynge	p 638, 658, i 295, 303, *Sacrament*	Sofre	p 257, 652, 739, ⎭
		Soget	p 49, *subject*

[69]

Soker	p 423, *succour*	Then	p 738, 780, u 46, &c., } *than*
Som	p 205, *some, all and some,* i.e. *one and all*	Thenne	p 210, 584,
		Thenne	p 171, 241, 319, & elsewhere *then*
Sonde	p 222, *sound*		
Sone	p 189, 464, 755, & elsewhere *sound*	Thenthe	p 201, *tenth*
		Ther	p 302, 353, *there*
Sothe	p 119, 221, *sooth, truth*	Tho	p 63, *then*, (Sax. *thonne*)
Sowles	p 258, *soul's*	Tho	u 5, *do, put*
Sowȝht	p 445, *sought*	Thowȝ	u 50, 56, *though*
Sowȝton	p 83, 85, *sought* (plural)	Thoȝght	p 517, *thought*
Spare	p 97, *forbear*	Threnteth	p 421, } *thirteenth*
Spende	p 766, u 74, *use, employ*	Threttene	p 239,
Spettyng	u 19, *spitting*	Throwȝ	p 377, 379,
Sportyn	p 65, *to disport*	Throȝ	p 53,
Spradde	p 36, *spread*	Throȝe	p 191, } *through*
Spylle	p 774, 399, *spoil*	Throȝgh	p 19, 29, 555,
Sqwyers	p 78, 413, *squires*	Throȝh	p 488,
Steven	p 613, *voice*, (Sax. *Stefnian* to call)	Thrydde	p 119, 275, and elsewhere, *third*
Stonde	p 101, 138, and elsewhere, *stand*	Thylke	p 183, 451, *the same, he that, they that*, (Sax. *thile* or *thillice*)
Straȝfte	p 72, *straight, directly*		
Strentbyn	p 68, *strengthen*	To	p 717, *too*
Stwarde	p 344, *steward*	Toke	p 146, 212, *took*
Stewardus	p 348, 350, *stewards*	Torne	p 285, *turn*
Style	u 87, *still, silent*	Toth	u 54, } *tooth*
Sum	p 16, i 302, } *some*	Tothe	p 746,
Summe	p 136, 308,	Towel	p 744, { the Italian *tovaglia* signifies *a table-cloth*, which is evidently the sense here intended.
Samtyme	p 145, *sometime*		
Suwe	u 83, *follow*, (see sewe)		
Sware	p 257, *oath*	Towelle	u 52,
Swythe	p 147, *very*		
Sycurly	p 18, 223, i 317, *securely, surely*	Towche	u 47, } *touch,* i.e. *help himself*
		Toyche	p 739,
Sye	p 527, *saw*	Trewthe	p 574, *truth*
Syens	p 556, 557, 573, & elsewhere *science, sciences*	Trw	p 521, } *true*
		Trwe	p 89, 337, &c.,
Syht	p 665, 676, 678, *sight*	Trwly	p 93, 103, &c., *truly*
Symplyst	p 39, *simplest*		
Syn	p 425, *see*	Uche	p 475, 677, 686, *each*
Syst	p 667, 753, 758, } *seest*	Uchon	p 41, 51, 81, and elsewhere *each one*
Syste	p 281,		
Syté	p 79, 412, *city*	Unbuxom	p 113, 451, *disobedient*
Syxte	p 161, 305, *sixth*	Unperfyt	p 155, *imperfect*
Syȝt	i 314, 327, } *sight*	Upryȝth	p 101, *upright*
Syȝte	i 335,		
Syȝth	u 74,	Vantage	p 149, 354, *advantage, profit*
Syȝth	p 398, *sees*	Voydance	u 20, *expulsion*
		Vyse	p 164, *wise, way,* i.e. *in any wise*
Take	p 420, *taken*	Vytayles	p 358, } *victuals*
Tawȝhte	p 57, } *taught*	Vytaylys	p 92,
Taȝghte	p 552,		
Techyn	p 14. 41, *to teach*	Walken	i 305, *walk*, (plural)
Tellus	p 590, *tells, says*	Warde	p 420, *ward, custody*
Thagh	p 748,	Wattryn	p 749, *to water*
Thaght	p 742,	Wende	p 715, u 23, i 300, *wend, go*
Thawgh	p 352,	Weren	p 514, *were* (plural)
Thawȝ	p 520, } *though*	Werkys	p 14, *works*
Thaȝgh	p 545,	Wes	p 35, 449, &c., *was*
Thaȝht	p 50,	Whad	p 445, *who,* (cf. Scot. *wha*)
Thaȝth	p 293,	Whar	p 388, *where*
The	p 359, 406, 585, & elsewhere *thee*	Wheche	p 28, *which*
		Where	p 473, *were*
The	p 724, u 32, *to thee, thrive, prosper*	Whether	p 99, 361, *whoever*
		Wod	p 520, *mad, furious*
Thef	p 180, 422, *thief*	Wol	p 1, 138, 178, &c., *will*

[70]

Wold	p 428, } would	Y-mad	p 359, 389, *made*
Wolde	p 158, 184, 259, &c.,	Y-meved	p 453, *moved*
Woldest	p 328, *wouldst*	Y-now3gh	p 316, *enough*
Wolen	p 388, } *will* (plural)	Y-ordent	p 297, } *ordained*
Wollen	p 372,	Y-ordeynt	p 261, 486,
Wolt	p 625, 760, *wilt*	Yoye	p 526, *joy*
Won	p 47, 139, 181, &c., *one*	Y-preved	p 455, *proved*
Worche	p 228, 270, 609, &c., *work*	Y-quelludo	p 182, *killed*
Wordyer	u 83, *worthier*	Y-ronne	p 537, *run*
Worschepe	p 34, 66, 192, } *worship, honour*	Y-schende	p 402, *spoiled, ruined*
Worsché	p 489,	Yse	p 692, *is*
Worththyur	p 737, *worthier*	Y-sette	p 731, *set down*
Woste	p 92, *knoweth*, (abb. of *wotest*)	Y-spoke	p 481, *spoken*
Wroghte	i 311, *wrought*	Ysse	p 119, 452, 573, *is*
Wro3ton	p 86, *wrought*, (plural)	Y-swore	p 436, 448, 483, *sworn*
Wryte	p 2, } *written*	Y-take	p 133, 199, 298, &c., } *taken*
Wryten	p 143, i 1,	Y-taken	p 336,
Wyl	p 442, *well*	Y-tolde	p 109, *told*
Wyl	p 566, 748, *will*	Y-wisse	p 4, 376, 451, &c., *I know*, i.e. *certainly*
Wylned	p 507, *willed, desired*		
Wyn	p 756, 788, *wine*	Y-worschepede	p 45, *reverenced*
Wynne	p 256, *win, gain*	Y-wryten	p 584, *written*
Wyse	p 55, *wise, manner*		
Wyste	p 550, *knew*	3af	p 24, 612, *gave*
Wyten	p 583, *to know* (Sax. *witan*)	3e	p 106, 126, 140, &c., *ye*
Wytte	p 29, 53, 83, *wit*, i.e. *knowledge*	3ef	p 33, 74, 133, &c., *if*
		3ef	p 305, *given*
Y	p 516, and elsewhere, *I*	3eke	p 283, *eke, also*
Y-bore	p 651, *born*	3er	p 60, 160, 175, & elsewhere *ere, before*
Y-bow3ht	p 358, *bought*		
Y-broke	p 482, *broken*	3er	p 122, 330, 472, 475, & elsewhere *year*
Y-callud	p 44, *called*		
Y-chasted	p 332, *chastised*	3eres	p 536, *years*
Y-clepede	p 46, *called, named, yclept*	3ese	p 141, *ease*
Y-cownterfetyd	p 22, *counterfeited, imitated*	3et	p 37, 43, 529, *yet*
Ydel	i 267, *idle, vain, senseless*	3eue	u 94, i 275, } *give*
Y-done	p 302, 466, 633, *done*	3eve	p 691, 790,
Y-dul	p 671, *idle, vain, senseless*	3every	p 232, *every*
Ye	i 325, *eye*	3onge	i 286, *young*
Y-ete	p 736, *eaten*	3or	p 640, *your*
Y-fere	p 4, 12, &c., *together*	3ow	p 61, 122, 178, *you*
Y-fonde	p 211, 487, } *found*	3owre	p 492, 577, 694, *your*
Y-fownde	p 443,	3urne	p 174, *soon*, (yrnan, Sax. *to run*. As *yerne*, immediately; Chaucer.)
Y-fownded	p 394, *founded*		
Y-holde	p 408, 471, *holden, held*		
Ylke	p 673, i 322, *ilk, same*	3yf	u 38, 68, 83, *if*
Y-lost	p 548, } *lost*	3yndynge	p 12, *ending, death*
Y-lore	p 652,	3ynge	p 639, *young*

COLOPHON

The Regius Poem

Three hundred and thirty-three copies of this limited edition were printed and bound by Pantagraph Printing Company of Bloomington, Illinois, from type set by that firm and from photoengravings made from the Quatuor Coronati Lodge No. 2076 copy of the Whymper facsimile edition of the original manuscript by Craske, Vaus and Crampton Ltd., photoengravers of London, England.

The type faces used for the type-set portion of the book are of the Linotype Janson and the Monotype Garamont families.

The text paper used is eighty pound basis ivory Colophon manufactured by the Curtis Paper Company. The book covers are made of Columbia Mills' Riverside Vellum over board and are stamped in genuine gold.

THE MATTHEW COOKE MANUSCRIPT

The following documents were not included with the original Masonic Book Club reprint of The Regius Poem (1970) and are included in this 2025 reprint as a bonus to our readers.

Like *The Regius Poem*, the bonus material comes from *Quatuor Coronati Antigrapha, Volume II* (London: Lodge Quatuor Coronati, No. 2076, 1890).

Honkyd be god
our glorious
ffadir and foun-
der and former of heuen
and of erthe, and of alle
thyngis that in hym is
that he wolde fochesaue of
his glorious god hed for to
make so mony thyngis of diuers vertu for mankynd.
ffor he made alle thyngis for
to be abedient & soget to man.
ffor alle thyngis that ben comes-
tible of holsome nature he
ordeyned hit for manys susty-
nauns. And allso he hath yif
to man wittys and connynge
of dyuers thyngys and craftys by the whiche we may
trauayle in this worlde to
gete w^t our lyuyng to make
diuers thingys to goddis ple-
sans and also for our ese and
profyt. The whiche thingis
if I scholde reherse hem hit
were to longe to telle and to
wryte, wherfor I wolle leue,
but I schalle schewe you some

that is to sey ho and in what
wyse the sciens of Gemetry
firste be ganne and whome
the founders therof and of
othur craftis mo as hit is notid in the bybille and in othur
stories.

OW and in what ma-
ner that this worthy
sciens of Gemetry began I
wole telle you as I sayde bifore, ye schalle vndirstonde
that ther ben VII liberalle sciens
by the wiche VII. alle sciens
and craftis in the worlde were
fyrste founde. and in especialle
for he is causer of alle. that is to
sey the sciens of Gemetry of alle
other that be. the whiche VII. sciens ben called thus. as for the
firste that is called fundament
of sciens his name is grammer
he techith a man ryzthfully to
speke and to write truly. The
seaunde is rethorik. and he techith a man to speke formabel-
ly and fayre. The thrid is
dioleticus. and that sciens techith

a man to discerne the trowthe
fro the fals and comenly it is
tellid art or sophistry. The fourth
ys callid arsmetryk the whiche
techith a man the crafte of
nowmbers for to rekyn and
to make a countis of alle thynge.
The fifte Gemetry the whiche
techith a man alle the mettis
and mesurs and ponderacion
of wyghtis of alle maner craftis.
The vj. is musikus that techith
a man the crafte of songe in
notys of voys and organe &

trompe and harp and of alle
othur perteynyng to hem. The
vij. is astronomy that techith
man the cours of the sonne
and of the moune and of other
storrys & planetys of heuen.
Wre entent is princi-
pally to trete of fyrst
fundacion of the worthe scyens
of Gemetry and we were
the founders therof as I seyde
by fore ther ben vij. liberalle
scyens that is to sey vij. sciens or
craftys that ben fre in hem

selfe the whiche vij. lyuen
onle by Gemetry. And Ge-
metry is as moche to sey
as the mesure of the erth
Et sic dicetur a geo qe quin R ter
a latine & metrona quod est
mensura. Una Gemetria in
mensura terre uel terrarum
that ys to sey in englische that
Gemetria is I seyd of geo that is
in gru. erthe. and metrona that is
to sey mesure. And thus is this
nam of Gemetria compovnyd
and is seyd the mesure of the erthe

Ervile ye not that I
seyd that alle sciens lyuen
alle only by the sciens of Gemetry. For ther is none artifici-
alle ne honcrafte that is wrozthe
by manys hond bot hit is
wrouzght by Gemetry. and a
notabulle cause. for if a man
worche with his hondis he worchyth with summe maner tole and
ther is none instrument of ma-
terialle thyngis in this worlde
but hit come of the kynde of
erthe and to erthe hit wole

turne ayen. and ther is non
instrument that is to sey a tole
to wirche with but hit hath
some porpocion more or lasse.
And proporcion is mesure
the tole er the instrument
is erthe. And Gemetry is
said the mesure of erthe where- 120
fore I may sey that men lyuen
alle by Gemetrye. For alle
men here in this worlde lyue
by the laboure of here hondys.
Ony mo probacions I
wole telle yow why that

Gemetry is the sciens that alle re=
sonable menn lyue by. but I
leue hit at this tyme for the longe
processe of wrytynge. And now 130
I wolle procede forthe on mi ma-
tere. ye schulle vnderstonde that
amonge alle the craftys of the
worlde of mannes crafte
masonry hath the moste no-
tabilite and moste parte of this
sciens Gemetry as hit is
notid and seyd in storialle
as in the bybylle and in the
master of stories And in poli- 140
cronico

a cronycle preuyd and in the
stories that is named Beda.
De Imagine mundi & Isodorus
ethomolegiarum. Methodius
episcopus & martiris. And other
meny mo seyd that masonsy is
principalle of Gemetry as
me thenkyth hit may welle
be sayd for hit was the fyrste
that was foundon as hit is
notid in the bybylle in the firste
boke of Genesis in the iiij.
chapter. And also alle the doc=
tours aforsayde acordeth therto

And summe of hem seythe hit
more openly and playnly
ryȝt as hit seithe. in the by=
bulle Genesis ~

Dam is line lynyalle
sone descendynge doune
the vij. age of adam byfore
noes flode ther was a mann that
was clepyd lameth, the
whiche hadde ij. wyffes the
on hyght ada & a nother
sella by the fyrste wyffe that
hyght ada, ho be gate ij. sonys
that one hyght Jobelle and the other

hight juballe The elderͤ sone
jobelle he was the first mann   170
that euer found gemetry and
masonry. and he mad how-
sis & namyd in the bybulle
Pater habitancium in tento-
riś atque pastorum That is to
sey fader of men dwellyng
in tentis that is dwellyng
howsis. A. he was caym is
master mason and gouernor
of alle his werkys whan   180
he mede the Citē of Enoche
that was the firste Cite

that was the first Cite that
euer was made and that made
Kayme Adam is sone. and
yaf to his owne sone Enoche
and yaff the Cyte the name
of his sone and kallyd hit
Enoche. and now hit is
callyd Effraym ad ther was   190
sciens of Gemetry and ma-
sonri fyrst occupied and
contrenyd for a sciens and
for a crafte and so we may
sey that hit was cavse & fun=
dacion of alle craftys and

sciens. And also this mann
Jobelle was callid Pater
Pastorum ~

The master of stories
seith and beda de yma-
gyne mundi policronicon &
other mo seyn that he was
the first that made deperceson
of lond that every man myght
knowe his owne grovnde
and laboure there on as for
his owne. And also he de-
partid flockys of schepe that
every man myght know his

owne schepe and so we may
sey that he was the first
founder of that sciens. And his
brother juballe. or tuballe
was ffounder of mysyke &
song as pictogoras seyth
in policronycon and the
same seythe ysodourus in his
ethemolegijs in the vj. boke
there he seyth that he was
the first foundere of Mysyke
and songe and of organ &
trompe and he founde that
sciens by the sowne of ponderacion

of his brotheris hamers that
was tubalcaym ~

Othely as the bybulle
seyth in the chapitre
that is to sey the iiij. of Genesis
that he seyth lameth gate apon
his other wiffe that hight sella
a sone & a dovcter the names of
them were clepid tubalcaym
that was the sone. & his doghter
hight neema & as the policronycon seyth that some men
sey that sche was noes wyffe
whether hit be so other no we afferme
hit not

IE schulle vnderstonde
that this sonne tubalcaym
was founder of smythis
crafte and of other craftys of
metelle that is to sey of eyron
of brasse of golde & of siluer
as some docturs seyn. & his
syster neema was fynder of
weuerscraft. for byfore that time
was no cloth weuyn but
they did spynne yerne and
knytte hit & made hem suche
clothyng as they couthe
but as that womann neema

founde that craft of weuynge
& therfore hit was kalled wo-
menys crafte. and thes iij.
brotheryn aforseyd had know-
lyche that god wolde take vengans for synne other by fyre
or watire and they had grete
care how they myʒt do to   260
saue the sciens that they founde
and they toke her conselle
to gedyr & by alle here witte
they seyde that were ij. maner of
stonn of suche vertu that the one
wolde neuer brenne & that stone

is callyd marbylle. & that other stoun
that wolle not synke in water, &
that stone is namyd lacerus. and
so they deuysyd to wryte alle   270
the sciens that they had ffounde in
this ij. stonys if that god wolde
take vengans by fyre that the
marbylle scholde not brenne
And yf god sende vengans
by water. that the other scholde not
droune. & so they prayed her
elder brother Jobelle that wold
make ij. pillers of thes ij.
stones that is to sey of marbll   280

and of lacerus and that he wolde
write in the ij. pylers alle
the sciens & crafte that alle they
had founde. and so he did
and therfor we may sey that
he was most connynge in
sciens for he fyrst bygan
& performed the end byfor
noes flode ~

Yndly knowyng of   290
that venganns that god
wolde sende whether hit
scholde be bi fyre or by water
the bretherne hadde hit not

by a maner of a prophecy they
wist that god wold send one ther
of. and therfor thei writen
here sciens in the ij. pilers
of stone. And summe men sey
that they writen in the stonis   300
alle the vij. sciens. but as
they in here mynde that a venganns sholde come. And
so hit was that god sende ven
ganns so that ther come suche
a flode that alle the worl was
drowned. and alle men were
dede therin saue viij. personis

And that was noe and his
wyffe and his iij. sonys &
here wyffes. of whiche iij
sones alle the worlde cam of.
and here namys were na-
myd in this maner. Sem. Cam.
& Japhet. And this flode was
kallyd noes flode ffor he &
his children were sauyd therin. And after this flode many
yeres as the cronycle telleth
thes ij. pillers were founde
& as the polycronicon seyth that
a grete clerke that called puto-
goras

fonde that one and hermes the
philisophre fonde that other. &
thei tought forthe the sciens that
thei fonde ther y wryten

A very cronycle and sto-
rialle and meny other
clerkys and the bybulle in principalle wittenes of the makynge
of the toure of babilon and hit
is writen in the bibulle Genesis
Cap Xº. hwo that Cam noes
sone gate nembrothe and he
wax a myghty man apon the
erthe and he wax a stronge

man like a Gyant and he was
a grete kynge. and the bygyn-
ynge of his kyngdom was
trew kyngdom of babilon and 340
arach. and archad. & calar &
the lond of sennare. And this
same Nembroth be gan the towre
of babilon and he taught and
he taught to his werkemen the
crafte of mesuri and he had
with hym mony masonys mo than
XL. thousand. and he louyd &
cheresched them welle. and hit
is wryten in policronicon and 350

in the master of stories and in
othere stories mo. and this a parte
wytnes bybulle in the same
X chapter where he seyth that a-
sure that was nye kynne to
Cam (Nembroth) yede owt of the londe of
senare and he brlled the Cite
Nunyve and plateas and other
mo thus he seyth ~ De terra illa
i. de sennare egressus est asure 360
& edificauit Nunyven & plateas civitate & cale & jesu quoque
inter nunyven & hec est Civitas
magna ~

Eson wolde that we schdde
telle opunly how & in
what maner that the charges
of masoncraft was first foun-
dyd & ho yaf fyrste the name
to hit of masonry. and ye
schylle knaw welle that hit told
and writen in policroycon &
in methodus episcopus and martiris
that asure that was a worthy lord
of sennare sende to nembroth
the kynge to sende hym masones
and workemen of craft that myghte
helpe hym to make his Cite
that he was in wylle to make.
And nembroth sende hym xxx
C. of masons. And when they
scholde go & sende hem forth. he
callyd hem byfor hym and seyd
to hem ye most go to my co-
syn asure to helpe hym to bilde
a cyte but loke that ye be welle
gouernyd and I schalle yeue
yow a charge profitable for
yow & me ~

When ye come to that lord
loke that ye be trewe to
hym lyke as ye wolde be to

me. and truly do your laboure
and craft and takyt resonabulle your mede therfor as ye
may deserue and also that ye
loue togedyr as ye were
bretheryn and holde togedyr
truly. & he that hath most conynge
teche hit to hys felaw and
louke ye gouerne you ayenst
yowr lord and amonge
yowrselfe. that I may haue
worchyppe and thonke for
me sendynge and techynge
you the crafte. and they res-
ceyued

the charge of hym that was here
maister and here lorde.. and
wente forthe to asure. &
bilde the cite of nunyve in
the countre of plateas and other
Cites mo that mealle cale
and jesen. that is a gret Cite
bi trene Cale and Nunyve
And in this maner the crafte
of masonry was fyrst prefer-
ryd & chargyd hit for a sciens.
Elders that were biforus
of masons had these
chargys wryten to hem as

we haue now in owre char
gys of the story of Enclidnis
as we haue seyn hem writen
in latyn & in frensche bothe
but ho that Enclyd come to gemetrye reson wolde we
scholde telle yow as hit ys
notid in the bybulle. & in othere
stories. In xij° Capitlo Genesis
he tellith how that abraham com to 430
the londe of Canan and owre
lord aperyd to hym and seyd I
schalle geue this lond to thi
seed. but ther fylle a grete hunger

in that londe. And abraham toke
sara his wiff with him and
yed into Egypte in pylgremage whyle the hungere du-
red he wolde byde ther. And A-
braham as the cronyculle seyth 440
he was a wyse man and a
grete clerke. And cowthe alle
the vij. sciens. and taughte
the egypcyans the sciens of
Gemetry. And this worthy
clerke Euclidnis was his
clerke and lerned of hym.
And he yaue the firste name

of Gemetry alle be that hit
was ocupied bifor hit had   450
no name of gemetry But
hit is seyd of ysodourus Ethe-
mologiarum in the v. boke. Ethe=
mologiarum Capitolo primo. seyth
that Euclyde was on of the firste
foundars of Gemetry &
he yaue hit name. ffor in
his tyme there was a wa=
ter in that lond of Egypt that
is callyd Nilo. and hit flowid 460
so ferre in to the londe that men
myght not dwelle therin

Hen this worthi
clerke Enclide taught
hem to make grete wallys
and diches to holde owt the
watyr. and he by Gemetry
mesured the londe and departyd hit in dyuers partys &
made euery man to close his   470
awne parte with walles and
diches and then hit became
a plentuos countre of alle
maner of freute and of yonge
peple of men and women
that ther was so myche pepulle

of younge frute that they couthe
not welle lyue. And the lordys
of the countre drew hem togedyr and made a conncelle   480
how they myght helpe here
childeryn that had no lyflode
compotente & abulle for to fynde
hem selfe and here childron
for they had so many. and
among hem alle in councelle
was this worthy clerke Encli=
dnis and when he sawe that
alle they couthe not brynge
a bout this mater. he seyd   490

to hem wolle ye take your sonys
in gouernanns & I schalle teche
hem suche a sciens that they
schylle lyue therby jentel
manly vndyr condicion that
ye wylle be swore to me to
perfourme the gouernanns that
I schalle sette you too and
hem bothe and the kynge
of the londe and alle the lordys   500
by one assent grauntyd therto.
          Eson wolde that every man
          wolde graunte to that
thynge that were profetable to him

self. and they toke here so
nys to enclide to gouerne
hem at his owne wylle &
he taught to hem the crafte
masonry and yaf hit the
name of Gemetry by cavse   510
of the partynge of the grounde that
he had taught to the peple
in the time of the makyng
of the wallys and diches a=
for sayd to clawse owt the
watyr. & Isodor seyth in his
Ethemolegies that Enclide
callith the craft Gemetrya

And ther this worthy clerke
yaf hit name and taught   520
hit the lordis sonys of the
londe that he had in his teching
And he yaf hem a charge that
they scholde calle here eche
other ffelowe & no nother-
wise by cavse that they were
alle of one crafte & of one
gentylle berthe bore. & lordis
sonys. And also he that were
most of connyng schold be   530
gouernour of the werke and
scholde be callyd maister &

othere chargys mo that ben
wryten in the boke of chargys And so they wrought
with lordys of the londe & made
citeis and tounys castelis
& templeis and lordis placis
Hat tyme that the chil-
dren of isrle dwellid 540
in egypte they lernyd the
craft of masonry. And
afturward they were
dryuen out of Egypte they
come into the londe of bihest
and is now callyd ierlem

and hit was ocupied & chargys y holde. And the makyng
of salomonis tempulle that
kynge Dauid began kynge 550
dauid louyd welle masons
and he yaf hem ryȝt nye
as they be nowe. And at the
makynge of the temple in
salomonis tyme as hit
is seyd in the bibulle in the
iij. boke of Regum in tercio
Regum. Capitolo quinto. That
Salomon had. iiij. score
thowsand masons at 560

his werke. And the kyngis
sone of Tyry was his master
masen. And in othere crony-
cleos hit is seyd & in olde
bokys of masonry that
Salomon confirmed the chargys that dauid his fadir had
yeue to masons. And salo-
mon hym self taught hem
here maners but lityll
defferans fro the maners
that now ben vsyd. And fro
thens this worthy sciens
was brought in to fraunce

And in to many other regions.
Umtyme ther was
a worthy kynge in
ffranns that was clepyd Ca
rolus secundus that ys to sey.
Charles the secunde. And this
Charlys was elyte kynge
of ffrauns by the grace of
god & by lynage also. And
summe men sey that he was
elite by fortune the whiche
is fals as by cronycle he
was of the kyngys blode
Ryal And this same kynge

Charlys was a mason
bifore that he was kynge. And
after that he was kynge he louyd
masons & cherschid them
and yaf hem chargys and
manerys at his devise the whiche
sum ben yet vsed in fraunce
and he ordeynyd that they
scholde haue a semly onys
in the yere and come and
speke togedyr and for to be
reuled by masters & felows
of alle thyngys amysse.
And sonne after that come

590

600

seynt ad habelle in to Englond
and he conuertyd seynt Albon
to cristendome. And seynt
Albon lovyd welle masons
and he yaf hem fyrst here
charges & maners fyrst
in Englond. And he or-
deyned conuenyent to pay
for ther trauayle And after
that was a worthy kynge
in Englond that was callyd
Athelstone and his yong-
est sone lovyd welle the
sciens of Gemetry. and

610

he wyst welle that hand craft
had the practyke of the sciens of Gemetry so welle
as masons wherefore he
drewe hym to conselle and lernyd practyke of that sciens
to his speculatyf. ffor of spec-
culatyfe he was a master
and he lovyd welle ma-
sonry. and masons. And
he bicome a mason hym-
selfe. And he yaf hem charge
and names as hit is now
vsyd in Englond and in
othere countres. And he
ordeyned that they schulde haue
resonabulle pay. And pur
chesed a fre patent of the kyng
that they schulde make a
sembly whan thei sawe re
sonably tyme a cum to gedir to
here counselle of the whiche
charges manors & semble
as is write and taught in the
boke of oure charges wher
for I leue hit at this tyme.
Ood men for this
cause and this maner

masonry tok firste begyn-
nynge hit befylle sumtyme
that grete lordis had not so
grete possessions that they
myghte not avaunce here
fre bigeton childeryn for   650
they had so many Therfore
they toke counselle howe they
myʒt here childeryn avaunce
and ordayne hem onestly to
lyue. And sende after wyse
maisters of the worthe sciens of Gemetry that ther thorou
here wysdome schold order-
                        ne

hem sum honest lyuyng.
Then on of them that had the   660
name wiche was callyd.
Englet that was most sotelle
& wise founder ordeyned
and art and callyd hit masonry. and so with his art honestly he thoʒt the childeren
of grete lordis bi the prayer of the fathers and the fre
wille of here children. the
wiche when thei tauʒt with   670
hie Cure bi a serteyn tymͤ
they were not alle jlike ab
                        lulle

for to take of the forseyde art
wherfore the forsayde maister
Englet ordeynet thei were
passyng of connynge schold
be passyng honoured And
ded to calle the connynge maister
for to enforme the lasse of connyng masters of the wiche   680
were callyd masters of no
bilite of witte and connynge
of that art Neuerthelesse thei com=
maundid that thei that were lasse
of witte schold not be callyd
seruante ner sogette but felaus

ffor nobilite of here gentylle
blode In this maner was the
forsayde art begunne . jn the
londe of Egypte bi the forsayd 690
maister Englat & so hit went
fro londe to londe and fro kyngdome to kyngdome after that ma
ny yeris in the tyme of kynge
adhelstone wiche was sum
tyme kynge of Englonde bi
his counselle and othere grete
tylle lordys of the londe bi comyn
assent for grete defavte y
founde amonge masons thei 700

ordeyned a certayne reule
a mongys hom on tyme of
the yere or in iij. yere as nede
were to the kynge and gret
lordys of the londe and alle the
comente fro provynce to provynce
and fro countre to countre
congregacions scholde be made
bi maisters of alle maisters
Masons and felaus in the
forsayde art. And so at suche
congregacions they that be mad
masters schold be examned
of the articuls after writen. &

be ransakyd whether thei be
abulle and kunnynge to the pro-
fytz of the lordys hem to serue
and to the honour of the forsaid
art and more ouer they schulde
receyue here charge that they
schulde welle and trewly dis-
pende the goodys of here lordis
and that as welle the lowist as the
hiest for they ben her lordys
for the tyme of whom thei take
here pay for here ceruyce
and for here trauayle. The
fyrste article ys this that euery

Maister of this art schulde be
wysse and trewe to the lorde that he 730
serueyth dispendyng his godis
trule as he wolde his awne
were dispendyd. and not yefe
more pay to no mason than
he wot he may diserue after the
derthe of korne & vytayle in the
countrey no fauour withstondyng
for euery mann to be rewardyd
after his trauayle The secund
article is this that euery master 740
of this art scholde be warned
by fore to cum to his congregacion
may asscusyd bi sume maner
cause. But neuerlesse if they
be founde rebelle at suche congregacions or fauty in eny
maner harme of here lordys
and repreue of this art thei
schulde not be excusyd in no 750
manere out take perelle of dethe
and thow they be in perylle of
dethe they schalle warne the
maister that is pryncipalle of the
gederynge of his dessese The
article is this that no master

take no prentes for lasse terme
than vij. yer at the lest by
cause whi suche as ben with in
lasse terme may not profitely
come to his art nor abulle
to serue truly his lorde to
take as a mason schulde
take The iiij. article is this
that no master for no profyte take
no prentis for to be lernyd
that is bore of bonde blode
for bi cause of his lorde to
whom he is bonde wolle take
hym as he welle may fro

his art & lede hym with hym out
of his logge or out of his
place that he worchyth in for
his felaus perauenter wolde helpe
hym and debate for hym. and
theroff manslaughter myzt
ryse hit is forbede. And also
for a nother cause of his art
hit toke benynynge of grete
lordis children frely begetyn
as hit is jseyd bi for The
v. article is thys that no master
yef more to his prentis in
tyme of his prentishode for

no prophite to be take than he
wote welle he may disserue
of the lorde that he seruith n̄ not
so moche that the lorde of the place
that he is taught jnne may
haue sum profyte bi his te-   790
chynge . The vi. article is
this that no master for no coue=
tyse nere profite take no prentis to teche that is vnprofyte that
is to sey havyng eny maym
for the whiche he may not
trewely worche as hym
ought for to do   The .vij.

article is this that no maister be
y foundė wittyngly or help   800
or procure to be mayntene &
susteyne any comyn nyʒtwal-
ker to robbe bi the whiche
maner of nyʒtwalkynge
thei may not fulfylle ther days
werke and traueyll thorow
the condicion here felaus myʒt
be made wrowthe   The .viij
article is this that yf hit befalle
that any mason that be perfite and 810
connynge come for to seche
werke and fynde any vnperfite

and vnkunnynge worchynge
the master of the place schalle receyue the perfite and do awey the
vnperfite to the profite of his lorde.
The ix. article is this that
no maister schalle supplant
a nother for hit is seyd in the
art of masonry that no man   820
scholde make ende so welle
of werke bigonne bi a no
ther to the profite of his lorde
as he bigan hit for to end
hit bi his maters or to whome
he scheweth his maters.

This councelle ys made bi dyuers lordys & maisters of
dyuers prouynces and diuers
congregacions of masonry   830
And hit is to wyte that who that
couetyth for to come to the
state of the forseyd art hit be
houeth hym fyrst princypally
to god and holy chyrche &
alle halowis and his master
and his felowis as his awne
brotheren. The secunde poynt
he most fulfylle his dayes
werke truly that he takyth for   840

that as welle the lowist as
as ᵹ the hiest schulde be welle
and trewely y-seruyd in
his art biforesayd thorow
out alle the kyngdomᵉ of
Englond. Amen so mote
hit be ~

———

THE MATTHEW COOKE, MS.

(Add. MS. 23,198, Brit. Museum.)

HIS Manuscript (of which a facsimile and transcript are prefixed) consists of forty folios of vellum, 4⅜ inches high and 3⅜ inches wide, of which the first three and the last two were originally blank. They are now defaced with writing, in a great measure illegible. On the first folio, however, is the name of "William K;" and again on folio 39. On folio 2 is written "Jno. Fenn, 1786," and we shall probably not err in assuming that these are the names of former owners of the manuscript. On folio 3, in the same handwriting as Jno. Fenn, is written "The Seven Sciences. Geometry. A History of Masonry. Its Articles, Points, etc.," being a very succinct index to the contents. Folio 2 also gives us as much of the history of the document as is known, for in the handwriting of Sir Frederick Madden, at that time keeper of the manuscripts, we read "Purch⁴ of Mrs. Caroline Baker, 14th Oct., 1859." The book is still bound in its two oak covers, and on each is the remains of a clasp, the hinged portion being missing.

There can be very little doubt that this was one of the manuscripts known to and utilized by Dr. Anderson, when he compiled the first Book of Constitutions in 1723; it certainly was known to prominent members of Grand Lodge in 1728, or five years later; for the Woodford MS. (now in possession of the Lodge), which is a copy of it, bears an inscription to the effect that it was made in 1728, by Wm. Reid, Grand Secretary, for Wm. Cowper, "Clerk of the Parliaments," who himself had been a Grand Secretary. It was, however, first brought prominently before the Craft by Bro. Matthew Cooke, who in 1861 edited a reproduction of it which was published by the late Mr. R. Spencer. This the only time it has been reprinted, and the execution is by no means perfect. The first page is given, as a frontispiece, in *facsimile*; but even this will not bear close inspection. The manuscript is then more or less successfully imitated in black-letter *type*, and contains not a few mis-readings. It would be ungracious to insist too much on these points, because the benefit conferred by Brothers Spencer and Cooke on the literature of the Craft was considerable and worthy of commendation. One error must, however, be noted, as it is of importance. At line 140 the editor has given us "And in policronico a cronycle *p'nyd*," and translated the last word *printed*; whereas it should be *p'uyd* or *preuyd*, i.e., *proved*, trustworthy. This error probably induced Bro. Cooke to ascribe the MS. to the "latter portion of the 15th century," as Caxton's edition of Policronicon was printed in 1482. It was admittedly the reason why Findel[1] concurred in this date, and subsequent writers have followed his lead.

Mr. E. A. Bond, late the principal librarian of the British Museum, gave it as his opinion that it was not later than the "first half of the 15th century."

Bro. Findel also made another very curious and even careless error. The MS. was purchased by the Museum from Mrs. Caroline Baker. In 1730 *circa*, Dr. Rawlinson wrote, "One of these rolls I have seen in the possession of Mr. Baker, a carpenter in Moorfields." Bro. Findel immediately jumped to the conclusion that this was the same manuscript, and called it the "Cooke-Baker document." But firstly, folio 2 would lead us to infer that in 1786 it belonged to Jno. Fenn, so that it is necessary to presume that 56 years after Rawlinson saw it, it passed out of Baker's possession, and then 75 years after that, was retransferred to a Mrs. Baker; and secondly, Rawlinson's document was a *roll* or scroll, and this is a book.

In concluding this description of its appearance and history, I will only add that the accompanying *facsimile* is the work of Mr. F. Compton Price, and will bear the most rigorous inspection and comparison with the original, whilst the sketch on the title page gives a very fair idea of its present outward aspect.

[1] History of Freemasonry, p. 31, London, 1869.

COMMENTARY.

ALTHOUGH the mere verbiage of the document presents so few difficulties that a glossary would appear scarcely necessary and almost an insult to the reader, and has therefore been omitted, yet the total absence of punctuation, the evidently inadvertent omission of a word here and there, and the faultiness of its grammatical construction, render it a difficult task to read intelligently. I have therefore ventured to give it here in in a modernised form, preserving strictly that which I believe it was the intention of the writer to convey. This plan will, I think, enable the reader to grasp its true meaning with great readiness, and to note, for comparison with other documents of a similar nature to be produced in future volumes of this series, certain peculiarities of much significance. The presence of the facsimile and transcript will enable the reader at all times to decide whether I have made undue inferences, and to correct my presentation by his own sounder judgment. Those of my readers who are fortunate enough to possess Bro. Hughan's "Old Charges of British Freemasons (1872)," which gives full transcripts of eleven of these documents, will be able to institute this interesting comparison at once: while the inclusion of two of them in the present Volume of Reprints will partially answer the same purpose.

THANKED be God, our glorious Father, the founder and creator of heaven and earth, and of all things that therein are, for that he has vouchsafed, of his glorious Godhead, to make so many things of manifold virtue for the use of mankind. For he made all things to be subject and obedient to man. All things eatable of a wholesome nature be ordained for man's sustenance. And moreover, he hath given to man wit and the knowledge of divers things and handicrafts, by the which we may labour in this world, in order to therewith get our livelihood, and fashion many objects, pleasant in the sight of God, to our own ease and profit. To rehearse all these matters here were too long in the writing or telling, I will therefore refrain; but I will nevertheless tell you some; for instance, how and in what manner the Science of Geometry was first invented, and who were the founders both thereof and of several other crafts, as is declared in the Bible and other histories.

How, and in what manner this worthy Science of Geometry took its rise, I will tell you, as I said before. You must know that there are seven liberal sciences, from which seven all other sciences and crafts in the world sprung; but especially is Geometry the first cause of all the other sciences, whatsoever they be.

These seven sciences are as follows:—

The first, which is called the foundation of all science, is grammar, which teacheth to write and speak correctly.

The second is rhetoric, which teaches us to speak elegantly.[1]

The third is dialectic, which teaches us to discern the true from the false, and it is usually called art or sophistry (logic).

The fourth is arithmetic, which instructs us in the science of numbers, to reckon, and to make accounts.

The fifth is Geometry, which teaches us all about mensuration, measures and weights, of all kinds of handicrafts.

The sixth is music, and that teaches the art of singing by notation for the voice, on the organ, trumpet, and harp, and of all things pertaining thereto.

The seventh is astronomy, which teaches us the course of the sun and of the moon and of the other stars and planets of heaven.

Our intent is to treat chiefly of the first foundation of Geometry and who[2] were the founders thereof. As I said before, there are seven liberal sciences, that is to say, seven

---

[1] *Formabely and fayre*, i.e., formally, according to form, and fair. [2] *We*, evidently a misreading for *whowe*.

The Matthew Cooke MS.

sciences or crafts that are free[1] in themselves, the which seven exist only through Geometry. And Geometry may be described as earth-mensuration, for Geometry is derived from *geo*, which is in Greek "earth," and *metrona*, or a measure. Thus is the word Geometry compounded and signifies the measure of the earth.

Marvel not because I said that all sciences exist only through the science of Geometry. For there is no art or handicraft wrought by man's hands that is not wrought by Geometry which is a chief factor (*notabulle cause*) thereof. For if a man work with his hands he employs some sort of tool, and there is no instrument of any material in this world which is not formed of some sort of earth (ore) and to earth it will return. And there is no instrument or tool to work with that has not some proportion, more or less. And proportion is measure, and the instrument or tool is earth. And Geometry is earth-mensuration, therefore I affirm that all men live by Geometry. For all men here in this world live by the labour of their hands.

Many more proofs could I give you that Geometry is the science by which all reasoning men live, but I refrain at this time, because the writing of it were a long process.

And now I will enter further into the matter. You must know that among all the crafts followed by man in this world, Masonry has the greatest renown and the largest share of this science of Geometry, as is stated in history, such as the Bible, and the Master of History,[2] and in the Policronicon, a well authenticated (or trustworthy) chronicle,[3] and in the history called Beda De Imagine Mundi, and Isodorus Ethomolegiarum Methodius Episcopus & Martiris. And many others say that Masonry is the chief part of Geometry, and so methinks it may well be said, for it was the first founded, as is stated in the Bible in the first book of Genesis and the fourth chapter. And moreover all the learned authors[4] above cited agree thereto. And some of them affirm it more openly and plainly, precisely as in Genesis in the Bible.

Before Noah's Flood, by direct male descent from Adam,[5] in the seventh generation, there lived a man called Lamech, who had two wives, called[6] Adah and Zillah. By the first wife, Adah, he begat two sons, Jabal and Jubal. The elder son Jabal was the first man that ever discovered geometry and masonry, and he made houses, and is called in the Bible the father of all men who dwell in tents or dwelling houses. And he was Cain's master mason and governor of the works when he built the city of Enoch, which was the first city ever made and was built by Cain, Adam's son, who gave it to his own son Enoch, and gave the city the name of his son and called it Enoch, and now it is known as Ephraim. And at that place was the Science of Geometry and Masonry first prosecuted and contrived as a science and as a handi-craft. And so we may well say that it is the first cause and foundation of all crafts and sciences. And also this man Jabel was called the father of shepherds.

The Master of History says, and Beda De Imagine Mundi, and the Policronicon and many others more say, that he was the first that made partition[7] of lands, in order that every man might know his own land and labour thereon for himself. And also he divided[8] flocks of sheep, that every man might know his own sheep, and so we may say that he was the inventor of that science.

And his brother Jubal or Tubal was the inventor of music and song, as Pythagoras states in Polycronicon, and the same says Isodorous. In his Ethemolegiis in the 6th book he says that he was the first founder of music and song, and of the organ and trumpet; and he discovered that science by the sound of the weights of his brother's, Tubal-Cain's, hammers.

And of a truth, as the Bible says, that is to say, in the fourth Chapter of Genesis, Lamech begat by his other wife Zillah a son and a daughter, and their names Tubal Cain, that was the son, and the daughter was called Naamah. And according to the Policronicon, some men say that she was Noah's wife; but whether this be so or not, we will not affirm.

Ye must know that this son Tubal Cain was the founder of the smith's craft and of other handicrafts dealing with metals, such as iron, brass, gold and silver as some learned writers say; and his sister Naamah discovered the craft of weaving, for before her time no cloth was woven, but they span yarn and knit it and made such clothing as they could. And as this woman Naamah invented the craft of weaving it was called woman's-craft.

And these four brethren knew that God would take vengeance for sin, either by fire or water. And they were much concerned how to save the sciences they had discovered, and they took counsel together and exercised all their wits. And they said there were two kinds of stone of such virtue that the one would not burn, called marble, and the other named "Lacerus" would not sink in water. And so they devised to write all the sciences they had found on

---

[1] This is the only document to my knowledge that applies the term "free" to the seven liberal sciences. If Masonry was a free (a liberal) science, were its professors therefore *free-masons*?
[2] Herodotus. [3] *cronycle preuyd*. [4] *doctours*. [5] *Adam his line lineal son descending*.
[6] *hyght*. [7] *departion*. [8] *departid*.

The Matthew Cooke MS.

these two stones, so that if God took vengeance by fire the marble would not burn, and if by water the other would not drown, and they besought their elder brother Jabal to make two pillars of these two stones, that is of marble and of "Laoerus," and to write on the two pillars all the sciences and crafts which they had found and he did so. And therefore we may say that he was the wisest in science, for he first began and carried out their purpose before Noah's flood.

Fortunately knowing of the vengeance that God would send, the brethren knew not[1] whether it would be by fire or water. They knew by a sort of prophecy that God would send one or the other, and therefore they wrote their sciences on the two pillars of stone. And some men say that they wrote on the stones all the seven sciences, but [this I affirm not].[2] As they had it in mind that a vengeance would come, so it befell that God did send vengeance, and there came such a flood that all the world was drowned and all men died save only eight persons. These were Noah and his wife and his three sons and their wives, of which sons all the world is descended, and they were named in this wise, Shem, Ham and Japhet. And this flood is called Noah's Flood, for he and his children were saved therein. And many years after the flood, according to the chronicle, these two pillars were found, and the chronicle says that a great clerk, Pythagoras, found the one, and Hermes the philosopher found the other, and they taught the sciences that they found written thereon.

Every chronicle and history and many other writers[3] and the Bible especially relate the building of the tower of Babel; and it is written in the Bible, Genesis, chap. x how that Ham, Noah's son, begat Nimrod, who grew a mighty man upon the earth and waxed strong, like unto a giant. He was a great king and the beginning of his kingdom was the kingdom of Babilon proper, and Erech and Accad and Calneh and the land of Shinar. And this same Ham began the tower of Babel and taught his workmen the Craft of Masonry,[4] and he had with him many masons, more than 40,000, and he loved and cherished them well. And it is written in Polycronicon, and in the Master of History, and in other histories, and beyond this the Bible witnesses in the same 10th chapter, as it is written, that Ashur who was of near kindred to Nimrod went forth from the land of Shinar and built the City of Nineveh and Plateas (sic) and many more. For it is written " De terra illa " [&c.]

It is but reasonable that we should plainly say how and in what manner the Charges of the Mason's Craft were first founded, and who first gave it the name of Masonry. And you must know that it is stated and written in the Polycronicon, and in Methodus Episcopus and Martiris that Ashur who was a worthy lord of Shinar sent to Nimrod the king to send him Masons and workmen of the Craft that they might help him make his city which he was minded to make. And Nimrod sent him 3000 masons. And as they were about to depart and go forth, he called them before him and said to them, " Ye must go to my cousin Ashur to help him build a city, but see to it, that ye be well governed, and I will give you a Charge that shall be to your and my profit.

"When you come to that lord, look that you be true to him, even as you would he to me, labour at your Craft honestly, and take a reasonable payment for it such as you may deserve. Love each other as though you were brothers and hold together staunchly. Let him that hath most skill teach his fellow, and be careful that your conduct amongst yourselves and towards your lord may be to my credit, that I may have thanks for sending you and teaching you the Craft." And they received the charge from him, being their lord and master, and went forth to Ashur and built the city of Nineveh in the country of Plateas (sic) and other cities also that are called Calah and Resen, which is a great city between Calah and Nineveh. And in this manner the Craft of Masonry was first instituted and charged as a science.

Elders[5] of Masons before our times[6] had these charges in writing as we have them now in our Charges of the story of Euclid, and as we have seen them written both in Latin and in French.

But it is only reasonable that we should tell you how Euclid came to the knowledge of Geometry, as stated in the Bible and in other histories. In the XIIth chapter of Genesis it is told how Abraham came to the land of Canaan and our Lord appeared unto him and said, "I will give this land to thy seed." But a great famine reigned in that land and Abraham took Sarah, his wife, with him and made a journey[7] into Egypt to abide there whilst the famine lasted. And Abraham, so says the chronicle, was a wise man and a learned.[8] And

---

[1] *hadde hit not.*
[2] I think the insertion of the above words is amply indicated. It makes sense which otherwise is very difficult to establish; it is justified by a similar remark at line 238; and it will be remembered that the brethren are not stated in the Bible to have discovered more than 4 crafts, of which only 3 are identical with some of the 7 liberal sciences; viz., geometry, arithmetic, and music.   [3] *Clerkys*
[4] *Mesuri. i.e.* mensuration.   [5] *i.e.*, Chiefs, superiors, masters or foremen.
[6] *" that were bi for us."*   [7] *pylgremage.*   [8] *grete clerke.*

The Matthew Cooke MS.

he knew[1] all the seven sciences and taught the Egyptians the science of Geometry. And this worthy clerk Euclid was his pupil and learned of him. And he first gave it the name of Geometry; although it was practised before his time, it had not acquired the name of Geometry. But it is said by Isodorus in the 5th Book and first Chapter of Ethomolegiarum that Euclid was one of the first founders of Geometry and gave it that name.

For in his time, the river of Egypt which is called the Nile so overflowed the land that no man could dwell therein. Then the worthy clerk Euclid taught them to make great walls and ditches to keep back the water, and by Geometry he measured the land and parcelled[2] it out into sections and caused every man to enclose his own portion with walls and ditches and thus it became a country abounding in all kinds of produce and of young people and of men and women: so that the youthful population[3] increased so much as to render earning a livelihood difficult. And the lords of the country drew together and took counsel how they might help their children who had no competent livelihood in order to provide for themselves and their children, for they had so many. And at the council amongst them was this worthy Clerk Euclid and when he saw that all of them could devise no remedy in the matter he said to them "Lay your orders upon your sons[4] and I will teach them a science by which they may live as gentlemen, under the condition that they shall be sworn to me to uphold the regulations that I shall lay upon them." And both they and the king of the country and all the lords agreed thereto with one consent.

It is but reasonable that every man should agree to that which tended to profit himself; and so they took their sons to Euclid to be ruled by him and he taught them the Craft of Masonry and gave it the name of Geometry on account of the parcelling out of the ground which he had taught the people at the time of making the walls and ditches, as aforesaid, to keep out the water. And Isodorus says in Ethomologies that Euclid called the craft Geometry.

And there this worthy clerk Euclid gave it a name and taught it to the lords' sons of that land whom he had as pupils.

And he gave them a charge. That they should call each other Fellow and no otherwise, they being all of one craft and of the same gentle birth, lords' sons. And also that the most skilful should be governor of the work and should be called master; and other charges besides, which are written in the Book of Charges. And so they worked for the lords of the land and built cities and towns, castles and temples and lords' palaces.

During the time that the children of Israel dwelt in Egypt they learned the craft of Masonry. And after they were driven out of Egypt they came into the promised land, which is now called Jerusalem, and they occupied that land and the charges were observed there. And [at] the making of Solomon's Temple which king David began, King David loved masons well, and gave them [wages] nearly as they are now. And at the making of the Temple in Solomon's time, as stated in the Bible in the third book of Kings and the fifth chapter, Solomon had four score thousand masons at work. And the son of the king of Tyre was his master mason. And in other chronicles and in old books of masonry, it is said that Solomon confirmed the charges that David his father had given to masons. And Solomon himself taught them their usages[5] differing but slightly from the customs now in use.

And from thence this worthy science was brought into France and into many other regions.

At one time there was a worthy king in France called Carolus Secundus, that is to say Charles the Second. And this Charles was elected king of France by the grace of God and also by right of descent.[6] And some men say he was elected by good fortune, which is false as by the chronicles he was of the blood royal. And this same king Charles was a mason before he became king. And after he was king he loved masons and cherished them and gave them charges and usages of his devising, of which some are yet in force in France; and he ordained that they should have an assembly once a year and come and speak together in order that the masters and fellows might regulate all things amiss.

And soon after that came St. Adhabelle into England and he converted St. Alban to Christianity. And St. Alban loved well masons and he was the first to give them charges and customs in England. And he ordained [wages] adequate to pay for their toil.

And after that there was a worthy king in England, called Athelstan, and his youngest son loved well the science of Geometry; and he knew well, as well as the masons themselves, that their handicraft was the practice of the science of Geometry. Therefore he drew to their councils (or took counsel, or lessons, of them) and learned the practical part of that science in addition to his theoretical (or book) knowledge.[7] For of the speculative part he was a master. And he loved well masonry and masons. And he became a mason himself. And he gave them charges and usages[8] such as are now customary in England and in

---

[1] *covthe.* [2] *departyd.* [3] *Myche pepulle of younge frute.*
[4] *take your sonys in gouernanns.* [5] *maners.* [6] *lynage.* [7] *speculatif.*
[8] *names*, evidently a mistake for *maners*.

The Matthew Cooke MS.

other countries. And he ordained that they should have reasonable pay. And he purchased a free patent of the king that they might hold an assembly at what time they thought reasonable and come together to consult. Of the which charges, usages and assembly it is written and taught in our Book of Charges; wherefore I leave it for the present.

Good men! for this cause and in this way Masonry first arose. It befell, once upon a time, that great lords had so many free begotten children[1] that their possessions were not extensive enough to provide for their future. Therefore they took counsel how to provide for their children and find them an honest livelihood. And they sent for wise masters of the worthy science of Geometry, that through their wisdom they might provide them with some honest living. Then one of them that was called Euclid, a most subtil and wise inventor[2] regulated [that science] and art and called it Masonry. And so in this art of his he honestly taught the children of great lords according to the desire of the fathers and the free consent of their children. And having taught them with great care for a certain time, they were not all alike capable of exercising the said art, wherefore the said master Euclid ordained that those that surpassed the others in skill should be honoured above the others. And [comman]ded to call the more skilful "master" and for [him] to instruct the less skilful. The which masters were called masters of nobility, of knowledge and skill in that art. Nevertheless they commanded that they that were of less knowledge should not be called servants or subjects, but fellows, on account of the nobility of their gentle blood. In this manner was the aforesaid art begun in the land of Egypt by the aforesaid master Euclid, and so it spread from country to country and from kingdom to kingdom.

Many years after, in the time of king Athelstan, sometime king of England, by common assent of his Council and other great lords of the land on account of great defects found amongst masons, a certain rule was ordained for them.

Once a year or every three years as might appear needful to the king and great lords of the land and all the comunity, congregations should be called by the masters from country to country and from province to province of all masters, masons and fellows in the said art. And at such congregations those that are made masters shall be examined in the articles hereafter written and be ransacked whether they be able and skilful in order to serve the lords to their profit and to the honour of the aforesaid art. And moreover they shall be charged to well and truly expend the goods of their lords, as well of the lowest as of the highest; for those are their lords for the time being of whom they take their pay in recompense of their service and toil.

The first article is this. That every master of this art should be wise, and true to the lord who employs him, expending his goods carefully as he would his own were expended; and not give more pay to any mason than he knows him to have earned, according to the dearth (or scarcity, and therefore price) of corn and victuals in the country, and this without favouritism, for every man is to be rewarded according to his work.

The second article is this. That every master of the art shall be warned beforehand to come to his congregation, in order that he may duly come there, unless he may [be] excused for some cause or other. But if he be found [*i.e.*, accused of being] rebellious at such congregation, or at fault in any way to his employer's harm or the reproach[3] of this art, he shall not be excused unless he be in peril of death.[4] And though he be in peril of death, yet must he give notice of his illness[5] to the master who is the president[6] of the gathering.

The [third] article is this. That no master take no apprentice for a shorter term than seven years at least, for the reason that such as have been bound a shorter time can not adequately learn their art, nor be able to truly serve their employer and earn the pay that a mason should.

The fourth article is this. That no master shall for any reward take as an apprentice a bondsman born, because his lord to whom he is a bondsman might take him, as he is entitled to, from his art and carry him away with him from out the Lodge, or out of the place he is working in. And because his fellows peradventure might help him and take his part, and thence manslaughter might arise; therefore it is forbidden. And there is another reason; because his art was begun by the freely begotten children of great lords, as aforesaid.

The fifth article is this. That no master shall pay more to his apprentice during the time of his apprenticeship, whatever profit he may take thereby, than he well knows him to have deserved of the lord that employs him; and not even quite so much, in order that the lord of the works where he is taught may have some profit by his being taught there.

The sixth article is this. That no master from covetousness or for gain shall accept an apprentice that is unprofitable; that is, having any maim (or defect) by reason of which he is incapable of doing a mason's proper work.

---

[1] *i.e.*, legitimate, not born of concubines or bondwoman. [2] *founder*.
[3] *repreue*, i.e. reproof. [4] *i.e.*, sick unto death. [5] *desesse*, i.e., dis-ease. [6] *pryncipalle*.

The Matthew Cooke MS.

The seventh article is this. That no master shall knowingly help or cause to be maintained and sustained any common nightwalker robber by which nightwalking they may be rendered incapable[1] of doing a fair day's work and toil: a condition of things by which their fellows might be made wrath.

The eighth article is this. Should it befall that a perfect and skilful mason come and apply for work and find one working who is incompetent and unskilful, the master of the place shall discharge the incompetent and engage the skilful one, to the advantage of the employer.

The ninth article is this. That no master shall supplant another. For it is said in the art of masonry that no man can so well complete a work, to the advantage of the lord, begun by another, as he who began it intending to end it[2] in accordance with his own plans, or [he] to whom he shows his plans.[3]

These regulations following were made by the lords (employers) and masters of divers provinces and divers congregations of masonry.

[First point] To wit: whosoever desires to become a mason,[4] it behoves him before all things to [love] God and the holy Church and all the Saints; and his master and fellows as his own brothers.

The second point. He must give a fair day's work for his pay.

The third [point]. He shall hele the counsel of his fellows in lodge and in chamber, and wherever masons meet.

The fourth point. He shall be no traitor to the art and do it no harm, nor conform to any enactments[5] against the art nor against the members thereof: but he shall maintain it in all honour to the best of his ability.

The fifth point. When he receives his pay he shall take it without murmuring, as may be arranged at the time by the master; and he shall fulfil the agreement regarding the hours of work and rest, as ordained and set by the master.

The sixth point. In case of disagreement between him and his fellows, he shall unquestioningly obey the master and be silent thereon at the bidding of his master, or of his master's warden in his master's absence, until the next following holiday and shall then settle the matter according to the verdict of his fellows; and not upon a work-day because of the hindrance[6] to the work and to the lord's interests.

The seventh point. He shall not covet the wife nor the daughter of his master or of his fellows unless it be in marriage, neither shall he hold concubines, on account of the discord this might create amongst them.

The eighth point. Should it befall him to be his master's warden, he shall be a true mediator[7] between his master and his fellows: and he shall be active in his master's absence, to the honour of his master and the profit of the lord who employs him.

The ninth point. If he be more wise and skilful than his fellow working with him in the Lodge or in any other place, and he perceive that for want of skill[8] he is about to spoil the stone upon which he is working and can teach him to improve the stone, he shall instruct and help him; so that love may increase the more amongst them and the work of his employer be not lost.

When the master and fellows, being forewarned, are come to such congregations, the sheriff of the country, or the mayor of the city, or alderman of the town in which the congregation is held, shall if need be, be fellow and associate of the master of the congregation, to help him against disobedient members[9] to maintain the rights of the realm.

And at the commencement of the proceedings, new men who have never been charged before are to be charged in this manner. Ye shall never be thieves nor thieves' maintainers, and shall do a fair day's work and toil for your pay that you take of the lord, and shall render true accounts to your fellows in all matters which should be accounted for to them, and love them as yourselves. And ye shall be true to the king of England and to the realm: and that ye keep with all your might and [power] all the aforesaid articles.[10]

After that an enquiry shall be held whether any master or fellow summoned to the meeting, have broken any of the beforesaid articles, which, if they have done, it shall be then and there adjudicated upon.

Therefore be it known; if any master or fellow being forewarned to come to the congregation, be contumacious[11] and appear not; or having trespassed against any of the aforesaid articles shall be convicted; he shall forswear his masonry and shall no longer exercise the craft. And if he presume so to do, the sheriff of the country in which he may be found

---

[1] probably through want of rest.   [2] *for to end hit.*   [3] *maters.*
[4] *to come to the state of the forseyd art.*
[5] *articles.* For my reasons for holding articles to be equivalent to legal enactments, see *post.*
[6] *lettynge,* i.e., prevention, hindrance.   [7] *mens.*   [8] *defawte of connyng.*   [9] *rebelles.*
[10] Notice that, the sheriff being present, thus constituting it a legal meeting, the articles only, and not the points, are mentioned.   [11] *rebelle.*

at work shall put him in prison and take all his goods for the use of the king, until his (the king's) grace be granted and showed him.

For this cause chiefly were these congregations ordained; that the lowest as well as the highest might be well and truly served in the aforesaid art throughout all the kingdom of England.

Amen, so mote it be.

The inferences derivable from a close examination of the MS. are of a highly interesting and, in some cases, of a rather startling nature.

The first point to be noted is, that the Add. MS. 23,198, is not an original document, but a transcript. It contains many orthographical and clerical errors which we should scarcely expect to find committed by a writer, if putting his own ideas on paper, but which are of constant occurrence in the case of a clerk copying from a document before him.

	At line	80	we find	we		for	whowe (who)
		118	,,	er		,,	or
		190		ad		,,	and
	,,	343		Nembroth			Cain (corrected by the scribe)
		496		ye			they
	,,	629		names		,,	maners
	,'	666		thoȝt			tauȝt
	,,	779		benynynge	,,		begynynge
	,,	892		perseyne			perseyne (perceive)

Most of these indicate the carelessness of a scribe copying mechanically and without attending to the sense of his words. Other orthographical errors I have taken no notice of, but there are many, some of which are noted in the paraphrase.

There are omissions, which tell more strongly still, as an author would naturally read over his work every now and then as he proceeds, and thus discover and rectify them, whereas a transcriber would go on, in blissful ignorance of having made a hash of the sense. Some instances are

	line	371	after	*hit*		insert	*is*
	,,	548		*and*		,,	*at*
		663		*ordeyned*			(probably) *that science*, for at present the *and* conjoins nothing
		755		*The*		,,	*third*
		835		,, *to*			*love*

Line 183 is a replica of line 182 and how this arose is evident. The clerk copied as far as "Cite that" and then looking to his original took up his next sentence at the first *that* instead of the second: a very frequent error of copyists. At line 344 he discovered a somewhat similar mistake and rectified it by erasure of the redundant words. The insertion of the word *tylle*, subsequently erased, at line 698 is curious, for it does not really occur in the MS. until line 950, where it is placed in exactly the same position on the page. Did the wind turn over several pages of the original? Some such accident seems the only plausible explanation of its insertion; but it is quite evident that the compiler himself would not have written it, for it is impossible to imagine any combination of words to succeed it which would make sense with those preceding.

The fact that the MS. is a copy, is perhaps more curious than important, because, although it points to the existence of an earlier original, this may not have preceded the instrument under consideration by many years. On the other hand it might be of much earlier date; but, inasmuch as the copyist would naturally, and unconsciously even, modernize the spelling, we can scarcely expect to decide that question by an examination of the version before us.

The original compiler was evidently anxious to exhibit his learning, as the constant reference to classic authorities indicates. This may be the effect of the pretensions of a literary quack or the harmless vanity of a really erudite man; but in any case, the author must have been of considerably better education than even a favourable specimen of a mediæval stonemason. Under these circumstances it is interesting and even important to gather from the MS. that he was himself a member of the Craft. The passages on which I base this conclusion are (line 418) "Elders that were bi for us of masons,"—implying that the writer was himself a mason and an elder of the craft; (line 421) "We have now in owre chargys;" (line 423), "We have seyn ham [*i.e.* the charges] writen in latyn and in Frensche bothe;" as it is scarcely to be presumed that a stranger to the Craft would have had access to so many copies. And again in lines 640-1, "taught in the boke of oure charges." Throughout the writer identifies himself with his audience, that is, the members of the Craft, and nowhere do I find the least indication to the contrary. He himself employs the term "speculative," and I shall, further on, consider in what sense he applied the word; but I think he fairly complies with the present definition of a "speculative mason."

Those who are tolerably acquainted with a few of the many known versions of the Manuscript Constitutions of Masons, will, on reading through the Matthew Cooke MS., at once recognize that down to line 638 the writer does not diverge in any great measure from the beaten track. But at this point, just where he should begin the rehearsal of the Athelstan Charges, he remarks—and the words are pregnant with great importance—"Of the whiche charges manors & semble as is write and taught in the boke of oure charges wher for I leue hit at this tyme." These concluding words distinctly imply that, not at this, but at some other time he will rehearse them.

At line 643 he begins afresh with the Euclid legend (omitting all the previous history) and in a condensed narrative carries us over the former ground to the point at which he left off, and then redeems his promise by reciting the full charges. This duplication of a part of the traditional history cannot fail to arrest our attention; and I shall show presently that we have here two distinct manuscripts, and that the first 642 lines only are the composition of the author; whilst the version from line 643 to the end, line 960, is of much older date.

The question at once arises, "who conjoined these two manuscripts: the author of the first, or the copyist?" The answer is equally ready. Not the copyist but the author himself, because had he broken off at line 642 he would have failed in his implied promise and left his story incomplete, nay, wanting its most important feature.

I shall now attempt to prove that this document consists of two distinct manuscripts and that the latter is the earlier. Inasmuch as they have both passed through the hands of a later transcriber, who, as I have already said, would inadvertently modernise the orthography; we should not look for any great and palpable difference between them. Yet even under these disadvantageous circumstances, some slight indications may perhaps exist. To properly pursue this line of research would require a more intimate acquaintance with early English writings than I can claim; but even to my inexperienced eyes, the verbiage of the second MS. appears rather more archaic than that of the first. It certainly gave me more trouble to construe, and that is a pretty good test. Again in the first 642 lines the Anglo-Saxon guttural g, written ȝ, only occurs four times; in the last 318 it recurs nine times, or nearly five times as often. In the first portion we have the word "Felowe"—in the latter it is written *Felau* eight times, *Felaw* twice, and *Felawe* thrice, and once only do we meet it as *Felows*. But there exists a still more convincing proof, to be referred to later, and which to my mind decides the question.

That the two parts are not by the same author is very obvious. To begin with, there is the difference of style. The one is diffused, the other curt, and even meagre. The first is interlarded with latin, and peppered with quotations and references to authorities, profane and divine; revealing at least a cultured, if somewhat pedantic, mind. The author attempts to argue and prove every point, and from line 81 to 130 we have a very curious sample of schoolman's logic. In plain words it amounts to this. Every craft works with tools. Every tool is made of some kind of earth or ore, and has some proportion or measure. Geometry means earth-mensuration. Therefore every craft is indebted to Geometry. And he winds up by stating that he could produce further proof of his proposition did time and space permit. Note also his attempt, at lines 580-588, to rebut previous writers and to prove that Charles Martel was no usurper. Now of this learned pedantry we find no trace in the second portion. We have not even a single reference to the Bible, much less to the classics. It is a plain straight-forward unvarnished tale, beginning abruptly with "Good men," and going to the pith of the matter, from which it never deviates, at once.

Then the author is very addicted to a particular form of address. The usual style in these MS. Constitutions is "Our intent is to tell you truly," and one instance of this is found at line 80. But at lines 40, 132, and 239 our author uses a phrase much more in consonance with his apparent character; "Ye schulle vnderstonde," which at line 371 he varies to "Ye schylle knaw welle." Of this phrase no sign is to be found in the second manuscript.

Another of his favourite words is "reasonable." We find it at lines 128, 633, and 637 in place of reasoning, fair, and fitting respectively. At line 395 he employs it very curiously, "takyt resonabulle your mede," meaning, as all the MS. Constitutions enable us to say, take your pay thankfully, without murmuring. The second portion uses the word "mekely" to render the same idea. And at lines 365, 426, and 502 we have the expression "Reason wolde that," signifying, it is but reasonable that. But in the whole of the second portion the word reason or reasonable does not occur once.

In the first portion the general gathering of the Masons is called "semly" and "semble" (lines 597, 639). This word is not once used in the second portion, but instead thereof we have, at lines 708, 712, 742, 830, 907, 939, and 953, "congregacion."

The Matthew Cooke MS.

Our author mentions Euclid several times, thrice as Enclidnis, once each as Enclyd and Enclyde, and thrice as Enclide. The substitution of n for u I attribute to the ignorance of the transcriber and the similarity of these two letters in old manuscripts. This word is therefore sufficiently correct to be the production of our learned brother. But in the second manuscript it is given as Englet and Englat (lines 662, 675, 691), a form which our author could not possibly have used, although it is found in other documents of the Craft. In the first portion he is invariably described as "that worthy clerk" (464, 487, 519), in the latter as "maister."

It is impossible to avoid the conclusion that we have in this document two distinct compilations; and further, that if the second was tacked on to the first by the author thereof, the second must necessarily have pre-existed, and is therefore of earlier date. That the writer knew of an earlier version of the Craft-legend is evident. I have already quoted lines 418-424, which assert that the story and charges of Euclid were possessed by former "Elders of Masons." At lines 534 and 641 he again alludes to the "Boke of Chargys." Taking these three passages together we learn the contents of this book of charges. It narrated the history of Euclid, and recited the charges of that worthy, and it dealt with the assembly ordered by Athelstan, and the charges and usages of the masons of that day. Now I am very desirous that my readers should refer to all these passages and carefully study the document as a whole, for it is a remarkable fact that nowhere does he indicate that the Boke of *Chargys* contained any thing else. Only one passage at first appears to contradict this positon and that is at lines 565-8, where he states that "old bokys of masonry" attest the fact that Solomon confirmed the charges of David. But our author here does not speak of *the* book, but of old books generally; still less is it the book of *Charges*, but books of *masonry*; probably works of architecture, if the books existed at all except in his imagination. Personally, I do not believe they did, otherwise he would have quoted the titles in full, and been only too glad of the opportunity to air his erudition. I believe we have here the earliest accurate description of the contents of the original Constitutions of the operative masons.

At the end of his manuscript, as already shown, he refrains from reciting the charges of Athelstan (or his son) *for "this tyme"*; evidently implying that he will give them later. And at the very next line he began to fulfil his promise, not by copying these charges out of the book, but by attaching to his manuscript the full text of a pre-existing document which was ready to his hand. That such was the case is, I think, now quite clear; and I almost venture to assume that he did not even take the trouble to re-write it, but simply tacked it on, or bound it up with his own. Otherwise he would scarcely have repeated the Euclid and Athelstan legends, all the more as the latter differs slightly from his own version; and being an educated man, he would not have contented himself with copying, but have left his personal impress on the document and assimilated its style to his own.

If my arguments thus far have obtained the concurrence of the reader, he will be by this time prepared for my next assertion, viz., that the second portion of Add. MS., 23,198 is neither more nor less than "the Boke of Chargys" itself. It agrees with the description contained in the body of the document, it conforms in every particular to what we should expect such a manuscript to be, it is curt, business-like, to the point; no portion of it is missing in the subsequent old Manuscript Constitutions, and finally, the most natural course for the author to pursue *was* to make use of "the boke of Chargys." I do not wish to assert that this MS. is the original book, or a copy of it, faithful in every particular, or even very much older than the first portion of the manuscript. It is probably not more than 50 or 60 years earlier than the author's time; but I do affirm that it is evidently the book in use among the masons of some particular part of the kingdom when and where our author was associating with them. And further than this, it is undoubtedly the purest, least altered copy of these Constitutions that has at present come down to us, and therefore the most valuable; far exceeding in intrinsic value the metrical version of it preserved to us in the Regius MS., No. 17, A.1; because less altered by poetical license. With two exceptions I believe it to be in all probability the exact counterpart of the first and original "Constitution." These are, first, the outer garb of language, which between, say the 12th and 15th centuries, altered very considerably; and secondly, it is possible that the original version began with king Athelstan, and that the legend of Euclid represents the first of a long series of embellishments applied throughout the ages to the laws of the Craft.

The Matthew Cooke MS., taken as a whole, consists then of a commentary, preceding a version of the "Old Charges." Subsequent rolls of the Constitutions make this commentary a part of the "Book" itself. Brother Gould is therefore right in placing this MS. apart from the others, because it is, as it were, an example of the transition state of this class of documents, and yet (as I hope to show), not their forerunner: but he is wrong in classing it with the Regius MS., from which it differs much more widely. Strike out from the manuscript the *repetition* of the Euclid and Athelstan histories (some 52 lines only), and it at once becomes a typical " roll of the Constitutions." But deprive it of the preliminary commentary, and it assumes its proper place, as the head of all the old Constitutions, the earliest, purest, and most important yet discovered.

I cannot help comparing our author to Dr. James Anderson, some 300 years later. Both found ready to their hands old documents, and each set to work to improve upon his originals; but with this difference: the one was enjoined to "digest" the old records into a method more befitting a new state of affairs, whilst his predecessor had probably no other motive than the honour of his craft and the instruction and pleasure of his fellows. Neither do I believe that he was the *first* embellisher, because somebody else had *perhaps* previously added the Euclid legend, and many copies of this version must have been in existence, for we see that the versifier of the Regius MS. had such an arrangement before him also, and in our author's days it formed an integral part of the "Boke;" and because, as I shall show, our author's own additions were evidently not all original and are *not* the source of more recent additions of the same tenour. The fashion of his time, and for 300 years afterwards, was to refine on the Craft-legend; he followed the stream, but by some accident was diverted into a backwater, and never reached the ocean, and what is absolutely original in his composition was never handed down and found no imitator.

Let me explain my position clearly. If the version under consideration had served as the basis for subsequent manuscripts, we should expect to find, in one or all of these every feature of the original, together with more or fewer further accretions. If in all subsequent manuscripts we find certain curious and important particulars missing, then these manuscripts do not derive, even indirectly, from the Matthew Cooke MS. If we find that the later versions and the Matthew Cooke MS. have, in spite of this, certain other features in common, we must assume that these are in both cases derived from a pre-existing common original. And such is really the case.[1] I will first point out some very remarkable passages which are not reproduced in later versions, but which are of such a nature that we can hardly imagine their being voluntarily omitted, knowing as we do that the tendency has always been to add more and more.

These are, the first 26 lines, dilating on the goodness of God; the definition of Geometry and its derivation (86-98); the schoolman's logic already referred to (99-125)[2]; the ingenious theory that Jubal discovered the *science* or theory of music from the ring and weight combined of his brother's hammers, the suggestion of a really scientific mind; the possibility of Naamah being Noah's wife (237); the description of the art of making clothing before Naamah's time (247-251); the fact that the brothers petitioned Jabal to make the pillars (287-280), and that it was he alone who wrote on them, thereby proving himself the most scientific of all the brothers (284-289); the suggestion that he wrote not only the four crafts but all the seven sciences (299-301); that Pythagoras found one of the pillars (322-3); the geographical description of Nimrod's kingdom (238-342); the defence of Charles Martel's legitimacy (584-9); the mention of St. Adhabelle (603)[3]; that Athelstan's son was a theoretical geometer or speculative mason before joining the Craft (624); and, finally, his references to classical authorities. As far as my recollection goes, not one of these points is treated of in the mediæval versions of the "Old Charges," and therefore I say that our author has not served as a model to subsequent writers.

On the other hand, much of the legendary lore in the Add. MS. 23,198 *was* embodied in later writings of the Craft, which proves that at least one contemporaneous or previous writer, from whom, or from whose congeners subsequent compilers copied, was known to our author. This gives us the measure of the amplification which the craft-legend had already undergone at that date. Amongst these must be reckoned the enumeration of the seven liberal sciences [also treated of in the Regius MS.]: the story of Lamech's children; of Noah's flood; of the tower of Babel (ascribed by the Regius MS. to Nebuchadnezzar and very shortly related), of Nimrod and Nineveh, Nimrod's charges, of Abraham in Egypt, of his pupil Euclid, of the straits to which the Egyptians were reduced by the plenitude of their fruitfulness (also given in the Regius MS.), Euclid's charges, David and Solomon's temple, of Charles Martel, of St. Alban, and of Athelstan's son. These additions to the original charges were evidently not known to the versifier of the Regius MS. with the exception of the three noted. Here we must suppose one of two causes. Either they were first added between the dates of the two documents, or more probably they took their rise in a district near our author and remote from the poet, to whose neighbourhood they had not yet

---

[1] I except, of course, one or two MSS. of the 18th century, which are avowedly copied from the Matthew Cooke MS. For instance, the Woodford MS., now in the possession of the Lodge.

[2] Other MSS. dilate on the superiority of Geometry, it is true, but not quite on the same grounds.

[3] This Saint is quite unknown. Dr. Plot laughs at Masons for their legend of St. Amphibalus, so some MS. or other must have contained the latter name. Are these two saints connected? The transcriber might possibly be answerable for the confusion.

percolated. But, according to my argument they must at some spot of England have been the common property of the Craft even before our author's time.

One further supposition may possibly be formulated. I think we may assume that that province or district which had so early elaborated to such an extent the original "Boke of Chargys," was ahead of all others, and that what was not current there was probably evolved at a later period of our history. To this class of additions belong Naymus Grecus, the assertion that St. Alban was a steward of the king's household, the name (Edwin) of Athelstan's son, the story that it was this Edwin who compiled the book of Charges, and the assigning to York the honour of being the seat of the first assembly. But this is only an inference, based upon less convincing premises than my other assertions; for it is quite possible that the York legend was current in that province much earlier and only found acceptance elsewhere gradually. But in any case we find by far the major part of the "Constitutions" as they descended to us in later documents, already the common property of at least one section of the Craft, at the date of the Add. MS. 23,198.

To put the matter concisely. We have three documents before us,—the Regius poem—the Cooke MS.—and a typical roll of the Constitutions,—of which the poem is acknowledged to be the oldest. We have also four classes of events mentioned, as follows

Class A is contained in all three documents, pointing to an earlier common original.

Class B is found *only* in the Cooke MS.—consequently these details are the compilation of the author of this instrument, and moreover, he has not served as a pattern for the later rolls.

Class C is contained in the Cooke MS., and in the Rolls, but not in the Regius. Therefore the original of the Cooke may have served the later scribes, but not the earlier versifier, pointing to a divergence of readings before the date of the poem.

Class D is found in the Rolls only, and is therefore of more recent date than the Cooke MS.

A Table would show it thus:—

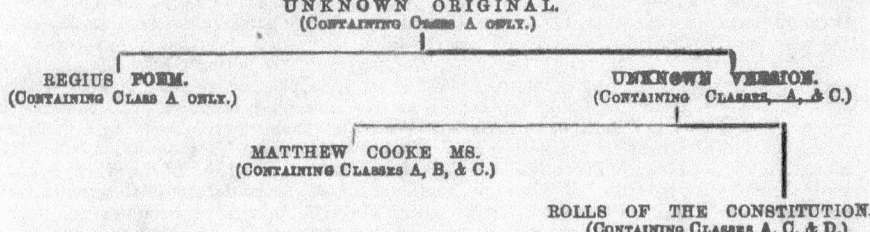

Many minor deductions follow from a minute study of the manuscript, but I will content myself by calling attention to one passage only; before passing to the consideration of the "Boke of Chargys" itself. At line 621 we read that Athelstan's son "lernyd practyke of that sciens to his speculatyf. For of speculatyf he was a master." In other words, he was a speculative mason. But we must be careful not to misunderstand the phrase or to jump to a hasty conclusion. To day a speculative mason is one who has been initiated into the rites of Freemasonry, even if not a mason by profession. It is put into sharp contrast with "operative," and the assumption is, that only in rare instances is a Freemason an operative mason *or in the least interested in real masonry*. The original meaning of "speculative" is hardly appreciated in our common use of the term. It was not so at the time of the revival in 1717 and for years after. At that time whole lodges were largely recruited from the ranks of operative masonry, and these members were operative Freemasons. The brothers of other professions admitted to their rites were speculative Freemasons, that is, they were Freemasons who *were* acquainted with the *art* in a speculative manner only, theoretically and by study; and old orations sufficiently demonstrate that all were expected (whether seriously or not) to make themselves theoretically acquainted with the science of Geometry and the practise of architecture. That this expectation was never (or rarely) seriously entertained, is beside the question; it was announced and the fiction covered and explained the use of the term speculative. But it is obvious that one could be a speculative *mason*, but not an accepted and speculative *Freemason*, without joining the fraternity; the means of architectural study existed outside the Lodge. This is exactly the position which our author assigns to Athelstan's son. Theoretically and by study, or *speculatively*, the prince had acquired a masterly knowledge of geometry and architecture, and for the sake of becoming practically acquainted with its application, he consorted with the masons and was made a mason himself. We thus see that in the 15th and again in the 18th century Masonic documents use the word in precisely the same sense; but the curious part is that intervening manuscripts reveal no trace of its usage. And yet, I believe, it was handed down amongst the masons, and not re-introduced fortuitously by Anderson or his co-temporaries, for the following reasons.

The original meaning of the word was the opposite of operative or practical; viz., *theoretical*, and as such we find it again used in the early years of the 18th century. Brother Gould, with his usual thoroughness, has collected nine examples of the use of the word in the intervening centuries, in many cases contrasted with the words *operative* and *practical*.[1] Of these, seven are directly connected with Geometry. Nevertheless, all this time the word was gradually losing its primitive significance of theoretical, until at this moment only a very correct writer would think of so applying it. It is no longer theoretical as opposed to practical, but intimates a process of inductive reasoning, an arguing from the known to the unknown. Thus a speculative merchant is one who forecasts the future of goods or prices from his knowledge of their present conditions, and stakes his fortunes on the result. A scientific speculation is a theory of unknown conditions based upon known facts. And in the centuries intervening, we see from Shakespeare, who uses the word as synonymous with thought or intelligence, that its primary meaning of theory opposed to practise had generally ceased to obtain

"Thou hast no speculation in those eyes
Which thou dost glare with."

Presuming that the masons in 1717 had to *find* or coin a word to express a non-operative mason, I cannot believe that they would have selected one to be used in a sense already practically obsolete; the coincidence would be truly remarkable. They would possibly have fallen back upon "theoretical," if left to themselves; but under the guidance of Dr. Anderson, I should expect to see introduced the old Scottish Masonic expression " geomatic." And no where else do we find " speculative " so used, except in Masonry: no other trade can produce a parallel. The amateur florist, the scientific agriculturist, the theoretical mathematician, the experimental chemist, as opposed to the gardener, farmer, accountant, or manufacturing chemist, do not, and never have, called themselves speculative. In spite of the failure of documentary evidence, I therefore believe that the Masons handed this word down amongst themselves, and that it is a genuine relic of antiquity.

We now come to the consideration of the second portion, or Boke of Chargys. That it did not at that time exist in one copy only, is proved by an examination of the first portion of the Regius MS. The versifier in that case must have had before him an almost identical document, for after making allowances for the redundancy of a poetic paraphrase, we shall find that these two MSS. are absolutely one and the same, except in certain particulars, which prove that the version given in Add. MS. 23,198 is of greater antiquity and therefore purer than that utilised by the poet, although the poem is earlier in date than the Matthew Cooke MS.

In both documents the introductory history consists only of the recital of the dearth of a suitable profession in Egypt, the intervention of Euclid, his charges, the arrival of the Craft in England in Athelstan's days (no mention is made of his son), and his charges, which are given at length and comprise the rest of the manuscript. Even peculiar expressions are preserved in the poem. Compare line 667, " bi the prayer of the fathers," with line 29 of the poem, " Throjgh fadrys prayers and modrys also." And again, line 685 *et seq.*, " Schold not be callyd seruante ncr sogette but felaus," with line 49, " Ny soget, ny servand."

With a comparison of the Articles and points my theory appears, but only momentarily so, in danger, because the poem recites fifteen of each and the prose version only nine. A more critical inspection reveals the fact that the additional clauses are such as would be necessitated by the extra experience gained in the lapse of years, and therefore proves the original of the poem to be a more recent version than that of the Cooke MS. Comparing the Articles in both versions we discover that,—

1. The master shall faithfully serve the lord, and not pay his workmen more than the price of victuals justifies;
2. That a master duly summoned shall not absent himself from the " congregation " without good excuse;
3. The prentice to be bound for seven years;
4. The prentice to be of free birth;
7. To harbour no thieves; and
8. To prefer the skilled workman to tho less skilled;

are practically the same, and often word for word identical.

[1] History of Freemasonry, II., p. 247.

The Matthew Cooke MS.

Article 5 of the prose version, not to pay the apprentice more than he fairly earns, is No. 6 in the Poem; and Article 6, to reject maimed candidates, is No. 5 of the Poem. The reason of this precept is given; because he could not do a fair days' work; and the Add. MS., or the oldest version, limits the " maim " expressly to causes which might incapacitate him in his work. In view of the absurd requirement which some Grand Lodges set up, that a candidate should be absolutely perfect, this " old landmark " is worthy of attention.

No. 9, no master shall supplant another, because obviously not so fitted to complete the work satisfactorily, is No. 10 of the Poem.

There remain Nos. 9, 11, 12, 13, 14, and 15 of the Poem to account for.

9. A master shall be proficient and be careful in laying his foundations. The first proviso may be gathered from the preamble to the charges in the prose version, and the second looks like an after enactment, the result of sorrowful experience.

11. Not to work at night: 12. Not to run down a fellow's work: 13. To complete the education of his apprentice: 14. To take no apprentice unless he have work to set him upon: and 15, not to take the part of his workmen when they are at fault, are all clearly later enactments, suggested by past occurrences and complaints that had been made. They prove that the rhymed version is from a later original than the prose.

Now let us turn our attention to the points.
1. To love God, the Church and ones fellow.
2. To give a fair day's work for the master's wage.
3. The mason must keep his master's and fellows' counsel.
4. And be faithful to the Craft.
5. And take his pay "mekely": *the master shall give timely warning that a man's services are no longer required.*
6. The settlement of disputes are to be remitted to a Holy or non-working day.
7. A mason shall not improperly desire his fellow's or master's wife, daughter, or concubine.
8. The warden shall be a true mediator between master and man.

All these are identical in both versions with the following slight exceptions. The italicised portion of No. 5 is found in the poem only and clearly points to a want which experience had shown to need a remedy. In No. 7 the prose version forbids concubinage, the rhymed one only prohibits unlawfully desiring a fellow's concubine. And in No. 8 the poem does not mention the warden by his title, but refers to him as having a "cure" or charge from his master.

No. 9 of the Cooke MS., that a more skilled craftsman should instruct the less skilled and avoid the possible waste of material, is the same as 11 of the Poem.

In the poem six further points are enumerated: but in the Add. MS. there follows after the 9th point a recapitulation or summary, and this contains five of these points. Thus No. 9 will be found practically at lines 921-5; 12 at 901-12; 13 at 915-17; 14 at 926-35; and 15 at 936-52. They therefore contain nothing new and with the exception of No. 9 are not *points* at all, as I shall show later on. No. 10, that no mason slander his fellow, is not provided for in the prose version except inferentially at line 925, " and hem love as hem selfe."

This portion of the *poem* concludes with a clause entitled " Alia ordinacio artis gemetriæ." This, with the exception of the last ten lines, in which Athelstan is apparently made to recite the very words of the charter in his own person, are however given in the preamble to Athelstan's charges of the prose version. We thus see that the poem contains nothing enumerated by the Cooke MS., except the additional articles already commented on, whilst every enactment and detail of the prose version is contained in the poem. This alone speaks strongly for the superior antiquity of the original on which the prose version is founded.

My comments have already run to such a length that I must not stop to point out the remarkable similarity in expression and verbiage between the two versions. Let the student, however, collate the two manuscripts, article for article, and point for point, and he will see how faithfully the poet has done his work. Even through the ornate garb of rhyme and rhythm, and in spite of the liberties thus rendered imperative, we are enabled clearly and certainly to identify the original text.

We are now arrived at the consideration of a most interesting question; the essential difference between the articles and the points. I shall content myself with referring to the later MS.: but will premise that the same arguments would apply to the Poem; the results to be deduced from either are identical.

Beginning at line 696 we read, that in Athelstan's time, by his counsel and that of the lords of the realm, by common assent, a rule was established for the masons. That, as might appear advisable to the king and his lords and the community in general, an assembly should be held every year or third year by the masters and fellows, at one place or another as might be needful. It then provides for the procedure at these congregations and recites

The Matthew Cooke MS.

the ARTICLES. Nowhere does it state that the masters assisted to formulate these articles, on the contrary, it states the rule (or rules) was made for them by the king and his lords. The articles were therefore a legal enactment, and the preamble and original nine probably contain the original clauses of Athelstan's charter, or, at least, of the charter which the masons, rightly or wrongly, ascribed to him. That these might be extended at future assemblies (as the Poem would lead us to suppose was done) is probable, because the chief representative of the king, in the province in which the assembly was held, was to be associated with the presiding master.

On the other hand, when we come to the points, line 827, we are no longer told that they were made at one time, but at divers times, in divers places, evidently as experience proved their necessity; and not by the King and his Council, but by employers (lords) and masters. They therefore had not the effect of law but were simple trade regulations. And the clauses themselves justify this inference in a remarkable manner. Every one of the nine *articles* is a political enactment, conducive to the welfare of the state, a police regulation, so to speak: and the six additional ones of the poem come under the same definition. Every one of the nine points is calculated for the good of the Craft or of the masters, and affects the state and employers only remotely. The addition to point 5 in the Poem is in favour of the workman; as are the added portions of Nos. 9 and 10.

At line 901 of the *prose* version, after point 9, the procedure to be observed at the assembly is continued, and the following lines contain the remaining four points of the *Poem*. Analogy would therefore lead us to infer that they are rather to be classed as legal enactments or *articles*, and this they are most evidently.

Point 12 provides that the provincial authorities shall render aid and assistance to the president, a proviso beyond the power of a mere trade assembly to lay down; 13, that no dishonest craftsman shall be employed; 14, that the masons shall swear to obey the ordinances, and to be liegemen to the king, and 15 establishes a correctional police to enforce the ordinance and articles. The *poet* was clearly wrong in calling these *points*: but neither are they *additional* articles, because the Boke of Chargys shows them to have been enacted in the first instance.

It has been generally assumed by Masonic writers of the old school that the Constitutions point to one general yearly assembly for the whole country, and that its place of meeting was York. The wording of this, the earliest Book of Charges, confutes this view. The assembly was to be held as necessity might arise when and where required, once a year or every third year as "nede were," and from province to province and country to country. That it was not held at any stated time or place is proved by the necessity of "warning" the masters and fellows (hence our "summons"); and line 742 speaks of "his" congregation, implying that there were different meetings for the different districts, otherwise the words would have been "the" congregation. In later documents a limit of distance is given, a mason living beyond the radius being excused, evidently a more recent enactment (comparable to our cable-tow), forced upon the Craft by experience. The distance varies from 5 miles to 100, and we can easily imagine that this arose from the great disparity in the extent of the districts controlled from one centre; or even, perhaps, the districts may have been extended as facilities of travel increased and roads improved.

This MS. also incidentally mentions a small and inevitable circumstance, curiously omitted in other and later MSS., viz., that the meeting was *presided* over by a master : "the maister that is pryncipalle of the gederynge," (line 754). He was virtually the Grand Master, for the time being, although the title did not really arise until 1717.

The meeting being duly assembled and graced by the presence of the Mayor, Alderman, or Sheriff, became invested with legal powers (901-912).

The FIRST business was to charge men that had never been charged before (912-14). It is impossible to read this otherwise than that apprentices who had served their time were here declared free of the craft, master workmen, admitted into the fellowship. In the 1723 Constitutions, Grand Lodge takes the place of these assemblies, and it was ordained that only at Grand Lodge should masons be received fellows and masters.

At the 2ND end of the meeting an enquiry was made (930), and this custom still obtains.

Many of the articles and points still find their counterparts in our present usages, but these are so obvious that I may be excused from pointing them out. It may be, however, convenient to summarize for easy reference the conclusions I have attempted to enforce. They are

1. The Add. MS. 23,198 is a copy of a pre-existing document, a transcript.
2. The compiler was himself a fellow-mason.
3. The compilation consists of two distinct documents,
   a. The compiler's commentary;
   b. A pre-existing document, tacked on in its integrity to the former, by the compiler himself.

4. The second part is the oldest and purest version yet come to light of the Book of Charges, or manuscript "Constitutions of Masonry."

5. This Book of Charges had already been enlarged and commented on by previous writers, and our author, to a certain defined extent, copied these.

6. He added further illustrations of his own.

7. His version has not served as the original of any other manuscript known to us.

8. Naymus Grecus, some of the particulars connected with St. Alban, Edwin's authorship of the Book, and the York legend, are of more recent origin.

9. The *preservation* of the word "speculative," in its present Masonic use, is to be ascribed to the Masons themselves alone.

10. At the date of this Manuscript there were several copies of the Book of Charges, identical with this one, in circulation.

11. The articles are legal enactments and had force as such.

12. The points are mere internal arrangements, of no strict legal value, yet enforced on all masons by the ordinary laws of guild life.

13. There was no one general assembly for the whole kingdom, but "congregations" were held when and where required.

14. That a Grand Master existed in fact, though not known by that name, and for the duration of each assembly only.

15. That the freedom of the Craft was conferred at these meetings only; and

16. That many of our present usages may be traced in their original form in this Manuscript.

G. W. SPETH, P.M., SECRETARY.

Related Titles from Westphalia Press

Ancient Mysteries and Modern Masonry: The Collected Writings of Jewel P. Lightfoot, Edited by Billy J. Hamilton Jr.

Jewel P. Lightfoot. Former Attorney General of the State of Texas. Past Grand Master of the Masonic Grand Lodge of Texas. From humble beginnings in rural Arkansas, he worked to become an educated man who excelled in law and Freemasonry. He was a gentleman of his time, well-known as a scholar, public speaker, and Masonic philosopher.

Essay on The Mysteries and the True Object of The Brotherhood of Freemasons
by Jason Williams

This isn't a reprint of a classic. It's a new rendition with new life breathed into it, to be enjoyed both by the layperson trying to understand the Craft and Masonic scholars taking a deeper dive into the fraternity's golden years—when the concepts of liberty and equality were still fresh.

Female Emancipation and Masonic Membership: An Essential Collection
By Guillermo De Los Reyes Heredia

Female Emancipation and Masonic Membership: An Essential Combination is a collection of essays on Freemasonry and gender that promotes a transatlantic discussion of the study of the history of women and Freemasonry and their contribution in different countries.

Freemasonry, Heir to the Enlightenment
by Cécile Révauger

Modern Freemasonry may have mythical roots in Solomon's time but is really the heir to the Enlightenment. Ever since the early eighteenth century freemasons have endeavored to convey the values of the Enlightenment in the cultural, political and religious fields, in Europe, the American colonies and the emerging United States.

Freemasonry: A French View
by Roger Dachez and Alain Bauer

Perhaps one should speak not of Freemasonry but of Freemasonries in the plural. In each country Masonic historiography has developed uniqueness. Two of the best known French Masonic scholars present their own view of the worldwide evolution and challenging mysteries of the fraternity over the centuries.

Worlds of Print: The Moral Imagination of an Informed Citizenry, 1734 to 1839
by John Slifko

John Slifko argues that freemasonry was representative and played an important role in a larger cultural transformation of literacy and helped articulate the moral imagination of an informed democratic citizenry via fast emerging worlds of print.

Why Thirty-Three?: Searching for Masonic Origins
by S. Brent Morris, PhD

What "high degrees" were in the United States before 1830? What were the activities of the Order of the Royal Secret, the precursor of the Scottish Rite? A complex organization with a lengthy pedigree like Freemasonry has many basic foundational questions waiting to be answered, and that's what this book does: answers questions.

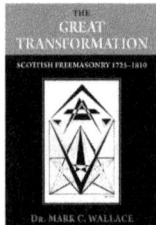

The Great Transformation: Scottish Freemasonry 1725-1810
by Dr. Mark C. Wallace

This book examines Scottish Freemasonry in its wider British and European contexts between the years 1725 and 1810. The Enlightenment effectively crafted the modern mason and propelled Freemasonry into a new era marked by growing membership and the creation of the Grand Lodge of Scotland.

Getting the Third Degree: Fraternalism, Freemasonry and History
Edited by Guillermo De Los Reyes and Paul Rich

As this engaging collection demonstrates, the doors being opened on the subject range from art history to political science to anthropology, as well as gender studies, sociology and more. The organizations discussed may insist on secrecy, but the research into them belies that.

A Place in the Lodge: Dr. Rob Morris, Freemasonry and the Order of the Eastern Star
by Nancy Stearns Theiss, PhD

Ridiculed as "petticoat masonry," critics of the Order of the Eastern Star did not deter Rob Morris' goal to establish a Masonic organization that included women as members. Morris carried the ideals of Freemasonry through a despairing time of American history.

Brought to Light: The Mysterious George Washington Masonic Cave
by Jason Williams MD

The George Washington Masonic Cave near Charles Town, West Virginia, contains a signature carving of George Washington dated 1748. This book painstakingly pieces together the chronicled events and real estate archives related to the cavern in order to sort out fact from fiction.

Dudley Wright: Writer, Truthseeker & Freemason
by John Belton

Dudley Wright (1868-1950) was an Englishman and professional journalist who took a universalist approach to the various great Truths of Life. He travelled though many religions in his life and wrote about them all, but was probably most at home with Islam.

History of the Grand Orient of Italy
Emanuela Locci, Editor

No book in Masonic literature upon the history of Italian Freemasonry has been edited in English up to now. This work consists of eight studies, covering a span from the Eighteenth Century to the end of the WWII, tracing through the story, the events and pursuits related to the Grand Orient of Italy.

westphaliapress.org

Policy Studies Organization

The Policy Studies Organization (PSO) is a publisher of academic journals and book series, sponsor of conferences, and producer of programs.

Policy Studies Organization publishes dozens of journals on a range of topics, such as European Policy Analysis, Journal of Elder Studies, Indian Politics & Polity, Journal of Critical Infrastructure Policy, and Popular Culture Review.

Additionally, Policy Studies Organization hosts numerous conferences. These conferences include the Middle East Dialogue, Space Education and Strategic Applications Conference, International Criminology Conference, Dupont Summit on Science, Technology and Environmental Policy, World Conference on Fraternalism, Freemasonry and History, and the Internet Policy & Politics Conference.

For more information on these projects, access videos of past events, and upcoming events, please visit us at:

www.ipsonet.org

www.ingramcontent.com/pod-product-compliance
Lightning Source LLC
Chambersburg PA
CBHW071714020426
42333CB00017B/2266